Dressage as art in competition

Dressage as Art in Competition

Blending Classical and Competitive Riding

John Winnett

THE LYONS PRESS
Guilford, Connecticut
An Imprint of The Globe Pequot Press

Contents

CONTENTS

List of Illustrations

List of Photographs

All photographs depict Greystoke, a Hanoverian gelding raised, trained and ridden by the author.

All photographs by Mary Magrane.

The Author

JOHN W. WINNETT WAS BORN IN LOS ANGELES IN 1928, was educated in Paris, France and lived and worked in Ceylon, India, England, and Germany.

Winnett moved to New York and, after a business career as a trader and member of the New York Stock Exchange, retired in 1970 in order to devote his full attention to training and competing with horses.

His equestrian career includes showjumping, eventing, steeplechasing, flat racing, polo, and dressage. He was also a breeder of Thoroughbreds for racing under the Valliere Farm name. His foundation mare Matriarch bred Rondeau, the champion two-year-old filly in the United States, and Targowice, the champion two-year-old colt in France.

To date, he has produced the following Grand Prix dressage horses: Khyber Pass, Poseidon, Sovereign, Mario, Hamadan, Arabella, Leopardi, Allegro, Highness, Amanasro, Fernet Branca, Greystoke, and Degen.

ACADEMIC TRAINING

1938—1940   M. Fradelle, Manege Montevidio, Paris, France (Basics)

1940—1946   M. Laurent, Manege, Montevidio, Paris, France (Dressage through the High School)

1946—1947   Centre National des Sports Equestre, Fontaine-bleau (Jumping and Cross-country)

1947—1952	Compte R. De Maille, Etrier, Paris, France (Jumping)
1968—1969	Fritz Steken, Tuxedo, NY (Dressage)
1969—1972	Dr. R. Klimke, Munster, West Germany (Dressage)
1972—1973	Peter Szalla, Warendorf, West Germany (Dressage)
1972—1978	H. Rehbein, Gronwohld Hof, West Germany (Dressage)

SOME HIGHLIGHTS OF HIS EQUESTRIAN CAREER

1945—	Junior National Champion of France (Showjumping)
1952—	Rode for USA in World Showjumping Championship
1972—	Rode in, and Captained USA Dressage Team (Munich Olympics)
1974—	Rode in, and Captained USA Dressage Team (World Championships, Copenhagen)
1975—	Rode in, and Captained USA Dressage Team (Pan American Games, Mexico)
1976—	Reserve rider USA Dressage Team (Montreal Olympics)
1977-1980—	Competed with distinction in national and interna - tional dressage shows throughout Europe
1980—	Rode in, and Captained USA Dressage Team (Moscow Olympics)
1981—	Olympic Festival (Individual Silver)
1982—	Olympic Festival (Team Gold)
1989—	Olympic Festival (Team Gold)
1990–Present—	Retired from international competition and stayed active as a trainer, instructor, and author.

METHOD AND THEORY OF TRAINING

Follows the principles of F.R. de la Guérinière, as understood by the Teutonic nations, supplemented by his own knowledge and study of biomechanics.

All of Mr. Winnett's horses show great suppleness, impulsion, lightness, and elegance.

Introduction to the
Second Edition

LOOKING BACK OVER THE TEN YEARS SINCE *Dressage as Art in Competition* was originally published, I can't find any revisions I wish to make in the basic fundamentals I wrote about back then. This should not be surprising, for the classic approach to training never changes. As the old saying goes: "Paris never changes; it is its citizens who do."

In this second edition I have added more detail and some updated material to several chapters. These additions are indicated in the text by footnotes, and can be found in the "Notes to the Second Edition" at the back of the book.

During these past ten years the United States has witnessed a steady growth in dressage. Progress has been made in all facets of the sport. We are still a very young nation and we have a way to go to catch up to the countries that in past centuries used dressage training for their very existence.

We are a very generous nation and have over the years welcomed many foreign horsemen to our shores. As a result, many different theories and methods from far-flung lands have found their way throughout our country. Some of these horsemen have contributed to American dressage; some have not. At best there is still confusion about the different approaches to training, especially among the less experienced trainers. We should, however, never be influenced by teachings that are not classical.

In essence, all methods of training are viable if they follow the laws of nature; however, none have been more successful than the teachings of François Robichon de la Guérinière, whose systematic method has been so successfully exploited by the Spanish Riding School and the German nation. Guérinière's method was lost in his native France during the French Revolution, and the Napoleonic wars which followed brought an end to the riding academies that had been sponsored by European courts familiar with his successes.

Max Ritter von Weyrother, head rider at the Spanish Riding School in the early part of the nineteenth century, is largely credited with introducing Guérinière's method to the school. His German disciples Seidler, Oeynhausen, and Seeger were later responsible for introducing Guérinière's teachings to Germany. Steinbrecht's book, *Das Gymnasium Dess Pferdes*, published in 1885, reflectes Guérinière's thoughts and is still the bible of the German School.

Almost every existing field of endeavor has expanded over the centuries. Classical equitation, however, still finds its fundamental roots in past centuries where the horse was everyone's friend, a necessary worker on the farm, a vital means of transportation, a partner in war, and an entertainer to the royal courts. It is no wonder that the horse held such importance in people's lives and drew the best minds of the time to continually find better ways to breed, train, and care for him. The old masters were kind enough to pass on their legacies and thoughts, almost all of which are still sound today!

Nearly all my thoughts are based on the theory of Guérinière. I have amplified my thinking on several aspects of training but have not wandered far beyond the domain of what is classical.

I hope this second edition will be helpful to all who wish to further their knowledge of training, riding, and competition. This book is the distillation of my sixty-seven years of experience and association with horses, which has encompassed breeding for racing, racing, polo, eventing, show jumping, and, lastly but not least of all, dressage.

—John Winnett

A Brief History of Classical Equitation

From xenophon to rome and the middle ages, to the Renaissance and the Neapolitan School in Naples, to the French School in Versailles; back again to Italy's Federico Caprilli, on to the Spanish Riding School and the institutions of Saumur and Hanover, the science of equitation has undergone many changes dictated by the necessities and needs of the times. Each century was a building link that made the whole chain possible. The link that without doubt contributed the most to equestrian science came out of the School of Versailles. Among all the great masters who appeared in succession during that prolific period, none stood higher than François Robichon de la Guérinière who, in 1733, wrote *Ecole De Cavalerie*. This book laid down the classical guidelines that have ever since given the riding masters and institutions that followed his teachings their successes. A study of la Guérinière's original text in Old French reveals in his own words that his innovations and method could not have been fully developed without the study of *Le Cavalerice François* published in 1594 by Solomon de la Broue who, along with Antoine de Pluvinel, brought the teachings of the Neapolitan School to France. La Guérinière also acknowledges through several passages in *Ecole de Cavalerie* his admiration for the writings of the Duke of Newcastle which greatly influenced his thinking and ultimately led to his invention of shoulder-in, the exercise that, in essence, revolutionized classical training.

The high collection, the creation of beauty and elegance through lateral bend of the horse's body, so explicit during the Versailles era, had to give way to the increasing need for and popularity of, cross-country riding. One of the first proponents of this new school was the Count d'Aure who in 1834 wrote *Traité D'Equitation*. This book endeavoured to show that while remaining loyal to classical principles, both manège and exterior equitation could be practiced successfully to their mutual development.

During this era François Baucher was practicing classical equitation at the highest levels of collection. Baucher introduced direct and lateral flexions of the horse's neck and jaw while dismounted. He worked his horses in double bridles and put great emphasis on lightness by working only one part of the horse at a time; a major departure from la Guérinière who emphasized working all parts of the horse 'in one piece' ('united') and together. Baucher finally, before his death in 1872, told his associate and student General L'Hotte, then the 'Grand Dieu of Saumur', that whenever and wherever difficulties occur with a horse they can only be cured permanently by use of a snaffle bridle. This radical change had little effect on his followers, who persisted in his methods of collection through use of a double bridle. A generation later James Fillis, following Baucher's method and through his own riding skills, performed incredible feats in the circus. Fillis also expanded on Baucher's method by acknowledging forward extensions and exterior equitation. Baucher's method was overshadowed by the growing interest in cross-country riding. His method nevertheless remained rooted in France and, through Fillis, spread to Russia.

Finally the classical principles of la Guérinière survived and were preserved by the Teutonic nations, especially Germany and Austria. From la Guérinière's thoughts emerged a classic German text, *Das Gymnasium Des Pferdes* by Gustav Steinbrecht, which still influences our thinking to this day. Steinbrecht's link with la Guérinière came through his teacher Louis Seeger, who ran a successful manège in Berlin and followed the teachings of la Guérinière.

Cross-country and jumping started to reach new heights of perfection at the Italian schools of Pinerolo and Tor Di Quinto through the efforts and genius of Federico Caprilli, whose method of exterior riding and invention of the forward jumping seat were exported with great success to all parts of the world.

Now poised at the door of the twentieth century, we enter the world of academic equitation, which encompasses high collection and extension to be reached through the gymnastic development of the horse's body. Jumping and cross-country riding developed on the basic laws and understanding of classical principles. This new art became a sport which reaches its pinnacle in competition at Olympic Games and World Championships. The history of modern equitation has received attention in many manuscripts, among which the most widely accepted in our present time are the works of General Albert Decarpentry, Colonel Alois Podhajsky and Waldemar Seunig. Without exception, these gentlemen remain loyal to la Guérinière in broad context.

The great masters of the past, who generously gave us their knowledge, were either training horses for the royal courts of Europe, the cavalries, or the circus. They were not asked to perform in competition against each other under a set of rigid rules in an arena surrounded by five critics who would eventually render judgment of their art, whether right or wrong! Performing in front of the public where accuracy is not *de rigueur*, is much easier than performing under competitive conditions.

CHAPTER 1

⌐—◦—⌐

The Rider's Seat and Posture

⌐—◦—⌐

I T IS IMPOSSIBLE TO RIDE WELL, OR TRAIN A HORSE unless the rider has a classic academic posture. Classic academic posture is not confined to one set position, but to a subtly changing series of postures. Each gait, each movement of the horse corresponds to a series of subtle postural adaptations by the rider. It is the ability of the rider to make such adaptations, rapidly and with suppleness, that constitutes what is often described as a 'classic seat'. To achieve this, the rider must acquire perfect balance on the seat bones, which in turn imparts feel and strength. The rider's upper body can be positioned in four ways; at the perpendicular, behind the perpendicular, forward of the perpendicular and side to side. When the upper body is kept at the perpendicular or slightly behind it, this allows the rider's seat bones to move forward (cantle – pommel direction) with the movement of the horse, allowing the rider to use the horse's strength against the horse. Imagine a cowboy coming out of a chute on a bucking horse. The rider leans back allowing the seat bones to go forward with the horse's motion. If the cowboy did not lean back, and tried staying seated with the strength of the legs only, the centrifugal force of the horse being much greater would throw the rider immediately to the ground. When the upper body leans forward of the perpendicular, the rider's seat bones work in the opposite direction (pommel – cantle direction) and against the motion and strength of the horse. There are times

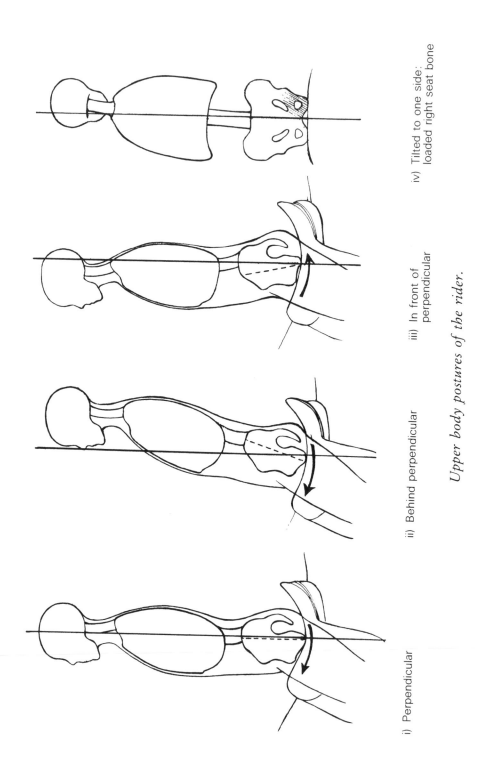

i) Perpendicular

ii) Behind perpendicular

iii) In front of perpendicular

iv) Tilted to one side: loaded right seat bone

Upper body postures of the rider.

when the rider must bring the upper body forward to relieve the horse's back of excess weight, for example when riding cross-country, when riding up and down hills, while galloping in suspension in the stirrups, and when jumping.

The rider's upper body can move side to side loading the inside seat bone when needed to follow the tilting of the horse's rib cage in lateral movements.

The rider's hands also play an important role in the academic posture. They have three objective positions: the neutral line, above the neutral line, and below it. The neutral line is a straight line from the rider's elbows through the forearms and reins to the horse's mouth. When the rider's hands are lifted slightly above the neutral line, the horse will drop his neck and head and 'chase' his bit down and forward. When the rider drops the hands slightly below the neutral line, the horse will lift his neck and head. This reaction to the hands seems somewhat illogical; however it is the natural reflex action of all horses.

No matter how good the rider's seat, there will always be a certain amount of motion imparted from the lower back to the hands. Therefore, the rider must always keep the hands together to allow them to work as one unit against body motion. The hands are used to the greatest effect when the wrists are slightly flexed to the inside and not held rigidly straight. This inside flexion allows more suppleness and lightness. When asking the horse for extension, the thumbs should touch. When asking for collection, the little fingers should come together. These two positions of the hands allow a great deal of longitudinal motion without having to displace the hands and while conserving the maximum diplomacy.

The rider's legs must fall naturally just behind the girth. The lower the thighs and knees on the saddle, the deeper the seat. The legs must not remain in constant strong contact on the horse, but remain steady in very light contact, and only be brought to bear when needed to influence the movement of the horse. The rider's heels must be flexed somewhat down and the toes held facing forward and as parallel as possible.

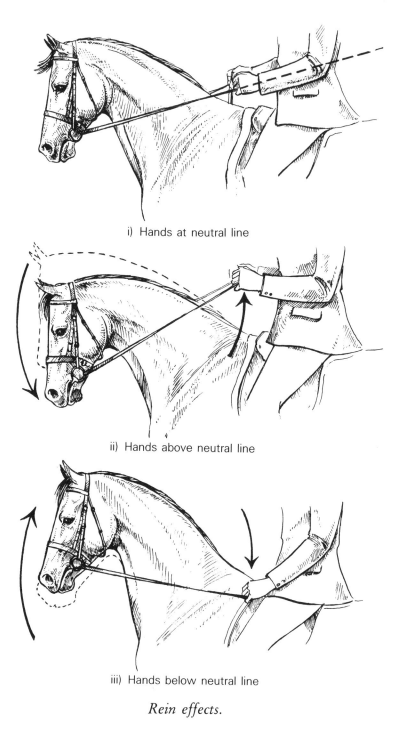

i) Hands at neutral line

ii) Hands above neutral line

iii) Hands below neutral line

Rein effects.

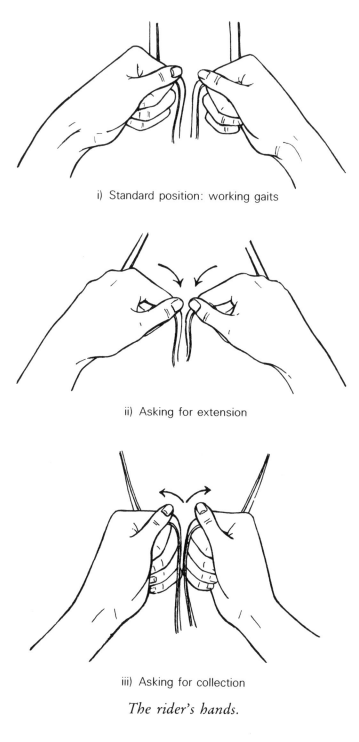

i) Standard position: working gaits

ii) Asking for extension

iii) Asking for collection

The rider's hands.

Exercises On Horseback

To find steadiness on horseback, the rider must acquire balance and security. Balance is acquired by riding without stirrups at the working trot and executing exercises in cadence with the gait without repercussion on the seat bones or lower back, which must remain slightly arched and supple to avoid stiffness. The trot is the gait which best imparts balance by virtue of its diagonal suspension.

Security is acquired by cantering without stirrups. This gait is also the best to promote strength cross-country over small jumps. Here are a few simple exercises that will help promote balance and security.

EXERCISES FOR THE LEGS

1) Detach the knees from the saddle. Lift the thighs horizontally, and put them back in place slowly.
2) Spread one thigh, bring the knee up to the horizontal, and give an energetic kick from front to rear. There must be no repercussion on the lower back, which must remain slightly arched. No stress must be placed on the front thigh.
3) Spread both thighs without bringing up the knees.
4) Slide one leg slightly behind the perpendicular, stretch the leg in the prolongation of the thigh. Rotate the heel outwards, and bring the thigh back into place without letting the knee come up.
5) Spread both legs laterally with toes raised, thighs and knees remaining fixed.
6) Bring one leg backward, knee remaining fixed, the heel flexed to the outside. Let the leg fall back to the vertical. The leg must oscillate back and forth like a bell clapper. In this exercise, the rider must acquire complete independence of leg and thigh.

During these exercises the rider must look high and forward to the front, avoid letting the seat slide back to the cantle, and keep his or her bust straight without hollowing the lower back.

EXERCISES FOR THE ARMS

1) Rotation of the arms backwards. Do not bend the elbows, and keep the fingers together and stretched.
2) Rotation of the arms in windmill fashion in both directions.
3) Rotation of the upper body, arms stretched in the prolongation of each other, hands shoulder high. Rotate the stretched arms and hips to the right and left, etc. The rider must keep the head up and turn it in harmony with arms and shoulders.
4) Flexion of one leg backward from fixed knee with rotation of opposite arm, without repercussion on the other leg or arm.
5) Bend upper body from the waist back and forth, and from side to side very fast, without moving seat bones in the saddle.

The first lessons should be given on the lunge line so that the student has only to concentrate on balance and the gymnastic exercises, while the instructor controls the horse's movement. As soon as the student has gained a fair amount of proficiency, the lunge lessons should be stopped in favour of free riding. If a student is kept for long periods on the lunge, there is a tendency to develop upper body crookedness and imbalance on the seat bones by constant turning on curves to the same direction. It is better for curves to be interrupted by straight lines, and then ridden in different directions on both reins. Another very important factor when riding without stirrups is to let the legs fall freely, with toes relaxed, in a downward position. This allows the rider to stay in balance on the seat bones without any interference from the legs, which would only create stiffness and loss of true balance. Obviously, when the rider needs to intervene with driving aids to influence the horse forward, or to turn on curves, the legs must be used, but the rider must bring them to bear with the toes down. This posture will keep the leg muscles relaxed and free from tension.*

*See Notes

Harmonization of the Aids

The following principles should be considered when seeking to achieve harmony of the aids.

HANDS WITHOUT LEGS — LEGS WITHOUT HANDS (DO NOT EXAGGERATE THE FORMULA)

When the hands act, the legs must cease their driving action, but they must 'hold' the horse. When the legs act the hands must cease their action, but they may resist. The legs impart impulsion. The hands regulate the impulsion. Legs and hands must assist each other by coordinating their effects to produce the gait, impulsion, collection, direction, or movement desired.

INTENSITY AND DURATION OF THE AID

Intensity of the aid. Act progressively in order not to go beyond the minimal intensity needed to obtain obedience.

Duration of the aid. Cease the aid as soon as the horse starts to obey. (It is a hindrance to ask a horse to turn when he is turning.) Most riders are inclined to do too much with their hands. Good hands are quiet hands and quiet hands result from a deep, strong seat and the ability of the rider to brace his or her back to follow the movement of the horse and drive the horse with the legs 'into' the hands, and onto the bit. The better the rider, the less the hands are used.

WEIGHT

The rider's weight may ultimately be considered the 'aid of aids'. Weight grows in importance with the horse's understanding and the intelligent use of the rider's buttocks, which, alone on a horse in self-carriage, must influence the motion in any direction. At this stage the rider's weight becomes a 'veritable aid'.

A sound classic posture is absolutely necessary in order to succeed in any equestrian discipline whether training or competing.

CHAPTER 2

——o——

Conformation and Choice of a Young Dressage Prospect

——o——

T HE FIRST THING I LOOK AT IS THE HORSE'S HEAD. 'There are no poker faces in the horse world' — at least among horses! I want to see a noble, sculptured head and bright, large eyes set well apart to indicate intelligence. The horse's eyes are very important to me; as in humans, they have a lot to reveal. If I do not like the eyes, I rarely look further. I also look for well-proportioned ears carried forward indicating alertness, nostrils that vibrate and show the character of respiration and a strong mouth and jaw to sustain the bit. A heavy head goes with a short, strong neck, while a light head needs a long, slim neck. A thick jowl will cause problems in collection and respiration. The proper proportion of the head and neck are very important for they effect the distribution of weight and the horse's ability to shift his centre of gravity. The brachiocephalic muscle provides a good indication of the horse's fitness and how well he can move his forelegs.

Standing in front of the horse, I look at the width of the shoulders and the distance between the forelegs at the level of the elbows. The chest must be large to hold the thorax. Forelegs set too close will pose real problems in lateral work. The rib cage should be streamlined. The scapula should be well-sloped. The

Greystoke. An eight-year-old Hanoverian gelding raised, trained and ridden by the author.

more sloping it is, the further back are the muscles which cover its outer surface and the better the freedom and movement of the forehand. The more upright the scapula, the more overloading of weight on the shoulders, and the more restricted the movement of the forehand.

Standing to the side I next look at the back. I want to see a good saddle position. High withers are an asset, provided they are covered with adequate muscle to either side, and taper away from above to below, providing a wide surface preventing the saddle from sliding forward. The back should be sufficiently wide to give the saddle comfortable support. The back should not be too short, which would restrict the fluid flow of a long elastic stride, nor too long, which could become a problem in higher collection. The haunches must not be higher than the withers, for this fault could not only cause poor balance, but could also become a real problem in the collected canter and all of its exercises.

The horse's elbows set directly below the shoulder joints usually go with an inclined scapula and short humerus, indicating speed and good gaits. Horses who have their elbows set too far back under the body usually have poor gaits. The optimum position of the elbows and withers ensures that the horse's girth is 2.5 centimetres behind the point of the elbow. Elbows that are set too far back increase the amount of concussion transmitted to the horse's spine. Any departure from the optimum position of the elbows will place extra strain upon the hocks, which will have to perform additional work to compensate for discrepancies in forearm action. The forelegs must be straight from elbow to fetlock. The hooves must be straight − never toed in or out.

Standing behind the horse I want to see both haunches level and equally developed. The thighs between the hind legs should almost touch, being rounded and full. A plumbline dropped from the point of the buttock should pass straight down the back of each hock and down the hind edge of each cannon. The hocks must be strong and straight; they must never be turned out (bow-legged). If the hocks are slightly turned in (cow hocked), I will overlook this fault for it can be of benefit in high collection, and in piaffe in particular. The hind legs must not be set too far apart. Horses with such conformation are harder to collect, and remain heavy on the rider's hands even after advanced training.

Movement

Once I have a general overall view of the horse's conformation, I want to judge his movement. I first have the horse walked in hand straight at me. Here I want to see the stifles remain in line with the body. The horse's legs must travel perfectly straight on two distinct tracks. I next view the horse walking away from me. Here I want to see him flex the fore and hind legs so that I can see the sole of each foot at the same position at each stride. I will, at the same time, observe the duration of each footfall. The horse will spend a fraction more time on his strong or, convex, side. If the horse is shod, I will examine the wear on each shoe, to give me further clues to straightness of movement and balance. I next view the horse from the side. Here I want to see the hocks flex to the same degree and to the exact same height. I also want to see 15 centimetres of overtracking and a clear four-beat rhythm. I will then have the horse's handler back him a few steps. Here I observe the action of the fetlocks, hocks, stifles and back. I want to see a clear diagonal rhythm with elevated straight steps.

After these examinations, it is time to observe the horse's trot and canter. Firstly, I always want to see the horse – especially a young prospect – move freely without the weight of a rider. This freedom of movement will give valuable clues as to what the horse will look like after training. In the free trot, I look for natural cadence of the hind legs, the engagement of the hip joints, length of stride and the level of the hocks. I want to see the forelegs move in perfect diagonal movement with the hind legs. The synchronization of the diagonal frame must remain in perfect rhythm. Of course the more brilliance and expression, the better. A word of caution – do not take note of the above gaits until the horse is quiet and moving with his natural impulsion.

In the canter, I look for clear three-beat rhythm, perfect synchronization of the transverse movement and, above all else, balance. Balance will give a good indication of the horse's potential scope over fences, as well as his ability to train to the highest levels of dressage. If the horse meets the above criteria, it is now time to observe him under saddle. Here, the only additional observations I will make are how well-proportioned the horse and rider are, how well the horse stays balanced under the weight of the rider and the degree of engagement and extension of the hind legs on straight lines and curves. I also want to observe a lot of natural impulsion. A lazy horse will never show enough brilliance at the higher levels of competition. I will then mount the horse for the final test – feel!

Where to Buy

I do not recommend buying horses at auction. One simply does not get to see enough of the real horse, and a clever auction rider can disguise problems. I will only buy horses from breeders and dealers who have well bred quality horses, and reputations for honesty and integrity. It goes without saying, the choice of a neutral veterinarian capable of making good x-rays, and furthermore capable of interpreting them, is of the utmost importance. Remember, four eyes are better than two, so take along a horseman who has had years of experience. His knowledge will be invaluable.

I have never found the perfect horse! You must remember in selecting a horse, that in training it is easier to overcome faults of conformation than faults of character. So when in doubt, have another look at the horse's eyes...

Breeding and the Genetic Pool

Breeding, genetics, and raising programmes are also very important factors in choosing a young prospect. Great horses are bred and raised, they do not come along by accident, and they are rarely raised under poor conditions. In Europe, especially in France and Germany, there are breeding programmes that have been followed for many generations. These systems allow the breed registries to maintain strict selections of stallions and mares, and to classify this breeding stock according to performance ability and breeding results. In short, the buyer has a 'Michelin Guide' at the fingertips to select the best genes for the end result desired, be it dressage, showjumping or eventing.

The vast majority of horses that have won or been placed in World Championships, European Championships, and Olympic Games, are related to certain identifiable bloodlines. These genes represent 10 per cent of the total genetic pool and constantly reproduce conformation, gaits, athletic and mental traits that lend themselves to the three disciplines. If you can find a horse that is bred from this small select genetic pool and has desirable traits you are looking for, you increase your chances of success considerably. Therefore, when looking for a young prospect, it is necessary to be familiar with the bloodlines, or to consult an expert who is.*

When I buy a young prospect I also want to know where he was raised and by whom. The important things to consider are

*See Notes

terrain, quality of grass and water, and management. The terrain should have good footing all year round, and not be too hilly for the weanlings, for fear of early stress on their fetlocks. As the weanlings become colts or fillies, they can be moved to more sloping terrain which will enhance their further development, their physical strength, lungs and heart. Limestone fields usually grow good grass, but the breeder or raiser who rotates the fields, takes bi-yearly soil samples for analysis, and limes and fertilizes the fields regularly, will greatly enhance the young horses physical development.

Management is a very important factor. Young horses must be properly handled from the very beginning of life. Proper hoof care, inoculations and worming programmes are of the utmost importance for the future good health of all horses. A scientific feeding programme, where vitamins and minerals are controlled and balanced, also adds to the likelihood of good development. Finally climate, although a lesser criterion, must be considered. A temperate climate without great extremities of heat or cold is most desirable.

Frozen Semen

Frozen semen, embryo transplants and cloning are surely the future of breeding. As I write this chapter in the last days of 1989, I firmly believe that this technology will be accepted in the next century. Genealogy is an exercise in statistics. It is therefore of the utmost importance to breed within the 10 per cent genetic pool in order to produce the best horses. Technology now allows us this possibility by breaking down geographic frontiers, time barriers, transportation and preservation. Over the last five years I have had the good fortune to consult and work with American Breeders Service, a division of W.R. Grace and Co. in DeForest, Wisconsin. This very able company and its research group have frozen semen from several stallions in my care with great success. I have bred mares with frozen semen only over this period and have obtained results equal to live cover. The advantages of this technology are obvious. For instance, a stallion involved in competition can have his semen collected in the off season and stored in liquid nitrogen to be ready for use during the normal breeding season without interrupting the stallion's training and show schedules. Stored frozen semen can also be used to continue a stallion's breeding season in the event of injury, illness, or death. Frozen semen can be shipped worldwide with no time restrictions, expanding the stallion's market and allowing breeders anywhere in the world to breed their mares to the foundation sires of the small select genetic pool I have mentioned. The advantages to mare owners of frozen semen breeding are also quite obvious. The mare does not have to leave home, thus saving the owner the cost of transportation and additional maintenance. The breeder is not subject to a tight time schedule as with fresh semen. The mare is protected against disease, and injury from the stallion. The breeder does not have to use an extender, or antibiotics, as these are already stored in the frozen semen capsule. By blood typing the stallions and mares, cheating and human error are virtually impossible. Frozen stallion semen will experience a very small decline in motility during the first two years of storage and will then stabilize and remain viable for fifty years, or probably a great many more, providing it remains properly immersed in liquid nitrogen (minus 197 degrees celsius).

As I write this chapter, embryo transplants and cloning are being researched in depth. It is now possible, under laboratory conditions, to split an embryo into thirty-two parts and grow thirty-two new embryos out of each split. Just imagine how fascinating it would be to own thirty-two identical horses and have them all trained by different trainers. Yes, I do believe we would experience results worthy of heated debate!

I have simply mentioned the advances in genetic engineering to point out the drastic changes, both economic and genetic, that will take place in sport horse breeding in the near future. The selection of a top dressage prospect will be much easier and cheaper than at present. This will widen the competitive base and in turn produce progress in our sport.

The passage of time has constantly seen scientific progress in the world. I would therefore have to conclude that genetic engineering will not be an exception, and will, in time, devise the means to complement and improve upon nature.

CHAPTER 3

⌐o¬

Psychology of the Horse and Its Use In Training

⌐o¬

IT WOULD BE PRESUMPTUOUS OF ME TO COVER this important subject from a scientific point of view, for I am not a Doctor of Psychology. I can only relate to the horse's behaviour from my long association with horses, and from scarce literary sources I have read on the matter.

My own understanding of the horse's behaviour revolves around his senses, memory, intelligence and reactions. I will cover each category in that order.

The Sixth Sense

⌐o¬

According to general acceptance, the horse has six senses: sight, hearing, smell, feel, voice and the much-debated sixth sense. The first five senses are more or less self-explanatory and I will come back to them later in this chapter. What is important in training is the horse's sixth sense. Some horsemen believe that this sense is psychic, while others dismiss the sixth sense as nonsense. I do believe that animals possess a sixth sense and I believe that Federico Tesio best observed it in his book *Breeding the Race Horse*. Tesio felt that the horse's ears serve purposes other than hearing: 'It would almost seem that they help sight-measure space.' He goes on to state, 'It is my belief the sixth sense of a horse can be compared to a radio, his ears serving as antennae, or to a divining rod which catches the radiations of water or metals hidden in the depths of the earth.' I would like to suggest that perhaps the horse's proprioceptive sense, which creates his balance and originates from the semicircular canals in his inner ear, could possibly have a relationship with Tesio's theory of radiation.

What we do know as horsemen is that horses can travel, without human assistance, in a straight line to sources of water situated at over thirty miles away in order to drink. When they lose their riders, they return to their stables by the shortest route without hesitation, from far distances without looking right, left, or stopping. They can move around in their stables in pitch black darkness without bumping into the walls and can take perfect aim at their mangers and water buckets without being able to see either. Horses can move and carry their riders in perfect balance cross-country on the darkest of nights. During World War II they were observed moving away to avoid bombs falling in their pastures.

I have recently made another puzzling observation. I have a wonderfully sensitive eight-year-old grey Hanoverian gelding who, on certain days refuses violently to pass under high-tension lines strung over a dirt road that leads to a flat field where we often work. I can only conclude that on certain days these lines emit an electrogenic activity which the horse is aware of and wishes to protect himself against at all costs.

Horses cannot see thirty miles away, they do not have night vision, and they cannot look up. From these observations we may deduce that the horse has a sixth sense, and until a qualified scientist comes up with a scientific explanation, I will go along with good old horse sense!

Memory and Intelligence

Memory and intelligence go hand-in-hand, for one cannot exist without the other. Every horseman agrees that horses possess an outstanding memory. In fact the horse's wonderful memory makes his training possible as we will discuss later. What is important to remember is that the horse records all direct associations in his memory bank; the good ones as well as the bad ones, and we can never remove these associations!

The horse's intelligence is much debated. Some horsemen feel that the horse is intelligent, while others tend to place the horse very low on the animal intelligence scale. I personally do not believe that horses are intelligent when assessed by the human definition of this quality; namely the ability to think abstractly as measured by objective criteria, or the skilled use of reason, or the ability to exercise good judgment based on sound thought. I do believe that when we associate the horse's senses, memory, and intelligence in one entity we can safely say that the horse is clever. Clever implies native ability or aptness, and suggests a lack of more substantial qualities. The horse is governed by direct associations of ideas, which are principally feelings of pleasure and discomfort. The horse is incapable of indirect associations of ideas based on intellect and reason.

Reactions

While in Paris during World War II, I observed horses in their stalls quietly munching their hay while a fifty millimetre anti-aircraft gun on the roof of a building across the street was firing round after round at a squadron of B-17 bombers trying to knock out the Renault factory a few miles away. The horses' direct association with this dangerous situation was that, since the noise did not hurt them, it could not be dangerous. In country stables I have observed horses pace around in their stalls and become lathered in their excitement for no apparent reason. Then all of a sudden, far away, faint sounds of horns and hounds could be heard by the human ear. In this case, the horses' primitive herding sense was awoken. The galloping sounds of the hunt horses scared the stabled horses into a frenzy, for the direct association of ideas warns them to join the herd and flee from the approaching danger. This natural phenomenon also explains why horses can be brought to safety out of a burning stable, only to run back into the flames and die. When a herd of wild horses is menaced by a prairie fire, their natural herding instinct guides them upwind through the flames to gain safety away from the moving fire. We may conclude that horses possess a keen sense of hearing well above human auditory limitations. Certain noises will have different effects on their minds.

Some years ago at the Aachen show in Germany, I was preparing to enter the competition arena on Sovereign, who was a very nervous horse, when the air raid sirens next to the stands started to blow. Sovereign jumped out of his skin, but settled down almost immediately as the deafening noise continued. The association of direct ideas was: terrible noise = scare = disobedience = continued noise = no pain = settle down. I could not hear the bell, but I could see the President of the Jury waving us on in, so we cantered in and performed one of the best Intermediate II tests of our careers. The loud noise of the siren dampened out the little or far away noises which often make a nervous horse very tense. The noise was so deafening I could not hear the applause from the grandstand, but as we rode by it on our way to the exit, I could see all the spectators standing and clapping. What a marvellous feeling for a rider! To make the morning even sweeter, the rider to follow us was one of the best in Germany, and unlike me, he refused to enter the arena until the sirens had stopped, which took a good five minutes. He got away with it because of who he was but when he finished his test, he was booed by the spectators! This man was not familiar with the psychology of the horse.

The Senses

The horse's exceptional hearing cannot be outshone by his sense of smell. Through the stimulation of his olfactory nerves, he is capable of puzzling reactions. A stallion can smell a mare in season from *very* far distances and react. I have often observed horses grazing in a field. They will come in turn to the same little patch of grass, smell it, and pass it over as unappetizing or dangerous. The same horses are fully capable of devouring poisonous weeds or leaves and dying. We must conclude that horses olfactory sense does not have the same power as their hearing perception, for it does not save their lives.

The horse's vision plays another very important part in training and can explain some of his reactions and behaviour. The horse's eyes are not frontal as in man, but oblique or lateral as in all animals that once had to survive in the marshes and plains. With this eye positioning, the horse is able to view two separate pictures at the same time to either side of his body. When the horse wishes to see a distant or near object in front of his body, he focuses both his eyes in telescopic manner on the object of interest. What is important to understand here is that the horse cannot use lateral and frontal vision at the same time. He can use one or the other separately. The horse can only focus his sight if allowed to move his head freely by raising, lowering or tilting it. In training, when we have the horse's head flexed in one position, removing any natural freedom of movement, we obviously obstruct the horse's ability to focus on objects. Horses are colour-blind and can only see different shades of grey, or changes in brightness. Very little information is, therefore, transferred to the horse's brain when he is at rest, or when objects around him are still, for there is little contrast in the dull shades of grey; however, as soon as the horse, or his surroundings, start to move, the movement will bring about changes in brightness, and the horse will recognize objects and their relationships to other fixed bodies. When the horse is moving toward a fixed object, his relative speed in relationship to the object will control the time of his reaction in terms of distance from the object. The faster his speed, the closer he will come to the object before registering a reaction. Some horses register more direct associations through their eyes than their brains can process; as a result they are highly strung, nervous, confused and tend to shy at unfamiliar objects.

As we have seen when discussing the horse's vision he reacts in four ways to an object of fear. His speed in relation to the object dictates at which point he will register fear and react. If he approaches the object straight on, his binocular vision leads him forward, and once in confidence with his rider, he will approach the object, and now being too close to focus, will smell the object for further evaluation. When approaching the same object from the side, one would think that the horse would have no objection to the object since he accepted it from a frontal view, but, not so — he will object. Now his lateral vision will take over, and it is necessary to make the horse confident to both sides of his body, for lateral vision only records one lateral view at a time on the object and, as stated, separately from frontal vision. When problems of shying and reactions to fear arise in training, it is best to allow the horse the free use of his neck and head to focus better on the object of fear.

Applying Equine Psychology to Training

Now that we have discussed the horse's senses, memory and intelligence, I would like to comment on them more directly in relation to training. As previously stated, I believe there is a sixth sense, and when a horse reacts for no apparent reason to unknown stimuli, the rider must not punish or force the horse's will, for one cannot effectively combat the unknown. Any rider who is lost in the woods on an overcast day has only to give the horse his head to soon find home! Never oppose the sixth sense; use it to advantage.

The horse's keen memory is the key to successful training. Like the elephant, the horse never forgets. While this is an asset, it also can be detrimental because the horse records both the good and the bad direct association of ideas. This fact is best observed in retraining spoiled horses. It is very difficult, if not sometimes impossible, to erase these bad impressions from the horse's memory. How then can direct associations be transmitted from the horse's brain to his memory? We cannot sit down with 'man's noblest conquest' and say, 'Now old man, this is what I want you to do — for the following reasons. If you do it well you will be rewarded for your efforts.' As previously stated, the horse does not have the ability to think abstractly as measured by objective criteria. His training must rely on direct contiguous associations which take the form of pain and pleasure administered by the trainer in the form of punishment and reward.

When a young horse starts his career in training he has natural sensitivity, especially on his bars and tongue, and to some degree on his flanks. It is up to the trainer to further sensitize these areas which are the major external sources of communication. The horses we are interested in for competition are warm- or hot-blooded, and possess more sensitivity than their cold-blooded peers. It would be difficult to train a Percheron with the same lightness of aids as a Thoroughbred. The trainer should always use a soft snaffle bit to obtain the utmost feel and sensitivity with the horse's mouth, and only use the double bridle to familiarize the horse with its action when it is called for in competition. 'If bridles had the miraculous propriety to make the horse's mouth, horsemen and horses would be skilful at the exit of a tack store!' – Pignatelli, 1580. If riding is feeling, then training is a hypersensitive reaction to the stimulation of feelings. The trainer's aids are the means of stimulation, the powers of persuasion, and yes, the pleasure of reward.

In order to communicate effectively with the horse, the rider's aids must be applied swïftly and with precision. The aids must intervene a split second before the mistake or disobedience occurs, and with an intensity proportionate to the horse's resistance, in order to allow the direct association to register. In some cases, it is necessary to repeat many contiguous associations until one association is indelibly registered on the horse's memory bank. The rewards must also be immediate, by giving with the hands and relaxing the leg aids, and praising the horse with the voice – if you were to come to a halt and fumble for a piece of sugar in your pocket, the horse would have no idea why he is being rewarded; the timing is lost. The horse's reaction to the direct association is: mistake = pain = obey = reward = pleasure. The horse will always follow his instinct for pleasure. The only time a trainer must follow a disobedience with a reward is when the horse is scared of an object: fear = praise = confidence. If the trainer were to punish a horse for showing fear, the direct association would be: punishment = greater fear.

The rider's aids must be deliberate and the horse must not be allowed to interpret kindness as weakness. In training, there is no room for brutality, but the horse must respect the rider, and maintain absolute obedience to and confidence in the rider's aids.

Greystoke with his handler, Judy Agusta. 'No amount of loving care will be too much in the stable'.

No amount of loving care will be too much in the stable. You can only ask the horse to give you as much as you give him. Horses become creatures of habit in their domestication. They submit willingly to the demands made upon them, providing they are treated intelligently by humans and accepted as friends. The horse always looks for leadership; he will therefore respect a strong and kind master.

I once was cussing out a horse for his stupidity, when one of my friends who was not familiar with horses asked me 'If this horse is so stupid, why do you spend so much of your time, money and efforts on him? It seems to me that you must be the dumb one...' By the way, this is not an old Arab proverb – it is a twentieth-century truth!

CHAPTER 4

—◦—

Biomechanical Action of the Vertebral Column, Thorax and 'Power Curve'

—◦—

B EFORE UNDERTAKING THE TRAINING OF HORSES, it is important to understand the simple biomechanical functions of the horse's body as well as the kinematic motion of some of the individual parts. Anatomically the horse is unsuited to perform the great feats we ask of him.

The evolution of the horse from his beginnings as a marsh-dwelling animal with five toes has not kept pace with the demands we make of him in modern times. The comparatively short time man and horse have been together is insufficient for the necessary evolutionary changes to develop. While the horse's body has changed dramatically over the ages, only further evolution can bring dramatic change in his performance.

The horse is a herbivorous animal, and his comparatively rigid spine is designed to support the enormous weight of his intestines. In contrast, carnivorous animals who hunt the herbivore all possess very flexible spines which allow them greater speed, jumping ability, and overall athletic prowess. By virtue of stamina, memory, and adaptability, the horse succeeds in performing most of what is asked of him with remarkable success. If we overload the horse's elaborate machinery by asking him to perform beyond his physical capability or degree of development, we will break him down. To understand the horse's limitations and advantages, it is necessary to understand the function of the vertebral column, thorax, and the 'power curve'.

The Vertebral Column

The vertebral column is divided into the cervical vertebrae (neck), the thoracic and lumbar vertebrae (back), the sacrum (croup) and the coccygeal (tail). The cervical can be easily flexed in just about all directions. The thoracic and lumbar are rigid with very limited movement. The sacrum does have some dorsoventral (upward and downward) movement thanks to the lumbosacral joint, any degree of spinal flexion taking place between the last thoracic and first lumbar vertebrae, between the first three lumbar bones and the lumbosacral junction. The coccygeal has little effect on locomotion other than indicating tenseness, stiffness, or relaxation by the position of the tail. The vertebral column is the axis upon which the limbs act to produce movement, and it will be flexed in various ways by forces produced by the hind legs pushing against the ground. The forces can be oblique, which flex the spine sideways, and vertical, which flex the spine upward. Sideways forces are produced by the oscillations of the hind legs forward and under to the medial line of the horse's body. These oscillations are very apparent at the walk. At the trot and canter, muscular resistance increases, making the column as rigid as possible, and eliminating sideways movement. Vertical forces increase the curvature of the spine and increase forward thrust.

L.B. Jeffcott of England and G. Dalin of Sweden, published in the *Equine Veterinary Journal* their clinical observations of the horse's spine that reveal that the overall increase of ventroflexion (collection) is 31.0 millimetres and dorsiflexion (extension) is 22.1 millimetres. Thus, the total range of movement in the dorsoventral directions of the spine is only 53.1 millimetres under experimental clinical conditions. The range of lateral movement and flexion of the spine is virtually non-existent. Any lateral bending of the spine begins at about the thirteenth thoracic vertebra (beneath the front of the saddle) and increases from that

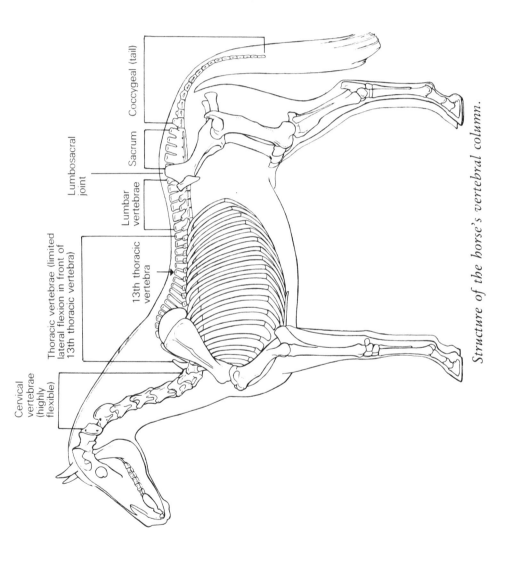

Cervical vertebrae (highly flexible)

Thoracic vertebrae (limited lateral flexion in front of 13th thoracic vertebra)

13th thoracic vertebra

Lumbar vertebrae

Lumbosacral joint

Sacrum

Coccygeal (tail)

Structure of the horse's vertebral column.

point forward. From these observations, it is obvious that the design of the horse's spine limits his ability to perform at high speed, over jumps, or bend his spine laterally.

The Thorax

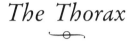

Since, in training we are concerned with lateral bend, we must understand the role of the thorax. The thorax is suspended between the two shoulder blades in the thoracic sling. This sling is not attached to the body by rigid connection, but by ligaments and muscles. The thorax has a great deal of movement within the sling and tilts by virtue of the motion of the horse's forelegs.

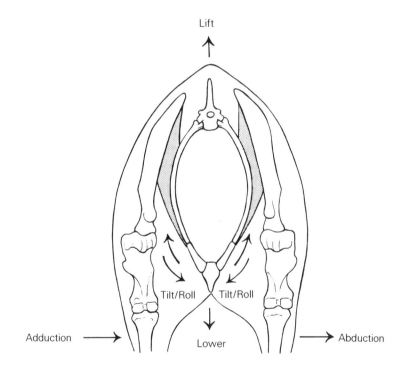

Diagram to illustrate the influences of the forelegs upon thoracic movement within the thoracic sling.

The thoracic sling and thoracic movement.

When a forelimb adducts towards the horse's body, this allows the thorax to roll over slightly in the thoracic sling in the direction of that leg. At the same time, the other forelimb abducts, or moves away from the body. Owing to the movement of the thorax in its muscle sling, the horse is able to move forward and sideways at the same time. It is this adduction and abduction of the forelegs that plays such an important role in dressage. The thorax may also be lifted and dropped very slightly in its seating at the same time as it tilts.

The 'Power Curve'

To understand this second motion of the thorax, it is necessary to refer to what I call the 'power curve'. This curve incorporates the action of the hindquarters on the horse's vertebral column and the role of the thorax on balance. The hind limbs can adduct, but they cannot abduct when in motion, because the accessory ligament limits their outward motion (this being a reason for limited speed). When the horse flexes his neck and poll, this increases the tension of the nuchal and supraspinous ligaments, which brings about the lifting of the thorax, shifting of balance to the rear, rounding of the back, tilting of the lumbosacral joint and the engagement of the hindquarters to the line of maximum lift (this is a perpendicular line through the point of the horse's hip to the ground). When the hindquarters engage to this line, the articulations of the three joints of the hind leg are coiled for maximum lift off the ground as in collection. On the other hand, when the neck is stretched out and lowered, and the muscles are relaxed and lengthened, the thorax then descends in its sling, shifts balance forward, and allows the hind legs to engage to the line of maximum thrust (this is a perpendicular line through the horse's centre to the ground. This point can be established by measuring a line from the point of the horse's hip to the point of his shoulder and dividing it in half). Where the hind legs engage to this line, the horse can exert maximum thrust and propulsion from the rear as in extension. Very rarely can a horse engage his hind legs beyond this line, because of the limiting action of the

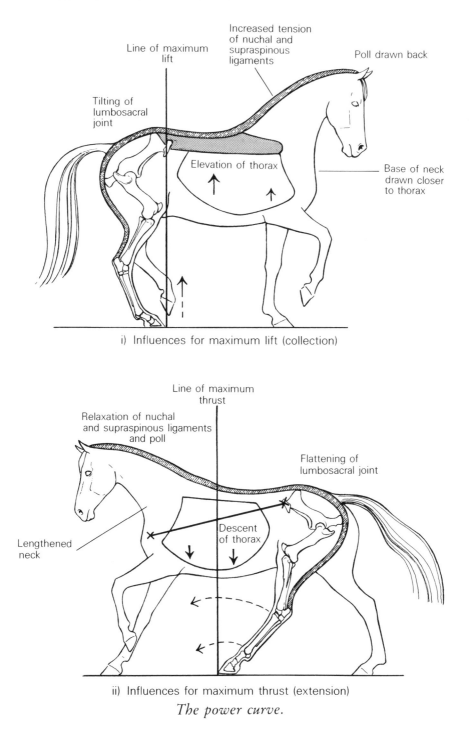

i) Influences for maximum lift (collection)

ii) Influences for maximum thrust (extension)

The power curve.

accessory ligament. The more the hind legs engage beyond the line of maximum lift, the more the horse's stride flattens and extends.

It should now be apparent that the horse cannot bend evenly from tail to poll as so many horsemen erroneously believe. However while he can bend his cervical vertebrae (neck) at will, and cannot bend his lumbar vertebrae (back) to any degree he can still bend geometrically. This is possible because he can rotate, lift and drop his thorax in the thoracic sling, and he can bend, or adduct his hind legs under to the medial line of his body. These observations should make it obvious that the horse's shoulders, and especially his hindquarters, must be made very supple through lateral gymnastic development. The horse's hind legs must be able to oscillate forward and under to compliment the tilting of the thorax and the lateral bend of the neck. Without complete suppleness of the hindquarters, there cannot be correct lateral bend.

Once the horse has reached a fair degree of lateral suppleness and strength in his shoulders and hindquarters, longitudinal suppleness will follow by virtue of the fact that the joints of the hind legs can now flex and oscillate to develop forward thrust to follow the lead of the forelegs, very much like a dancing partner. At this stage the horse is able to place himself on the 'power curve' required to create forward or upward thrust and increased balance.

Balance can be improved, but it cannot be created in training. It is dependent on the horse's proprioceptive sense. This provides the horse with information which enables him to decide whether he is right side up, or upside down, or indeed out of balance. The proprioceptive sense is closely associated with the horse's internal ear and its semicircular canals. The degree of development of this sense is acquired through genetic inheritance.*

*See Notes

CHAPTER 5

Rectitude of the Horse

THE TERM RECTITUDE IS EMPLOYED HERE, and throughout the text to describe 'straightness' as understood by students of equitation. In order to achieve this, a trainer must work towards the even development of the muscles on both sides of the horse's body.

Like man, the horse is born with a weak and strong side, and like man, the horse's right side is generally stronger. As a result, the horse's body will be convex to the dominant side and he will carry most of his weight on the right lateral. The horse avoids, as much as possible, loading weight onto his weak and concave left lateral, and reduces the duration of pose on that side, hastily loading his right legs. As a result, the right lateral lacks suppleness and flexibility, and the undulations of the spine are not symmetric or even. In the walk, the horse's neck remains incurvated to the left; he resists the action of the right rein and gives too easily to the left rein, without stretching into it on straight lines. Therefore, irregularities of gait are observed, especially in the hindquarters: the horse has difficulty engaging his left hip joint due to the lack of thrust from the right hind leg. While on a circle to the right, he does not stretch into the right rein because of his convexity to that side, and the consequent tendency to shift weight onto the dominant lateral. Furthermore, the right hind leg being stronger and stiffer causes the haunches to deviate to the outside of the circle, reducing engagement of

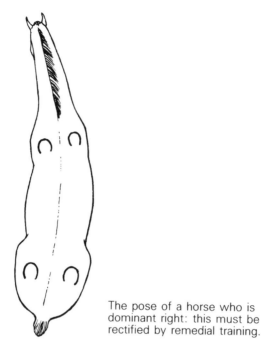

The pose of a horse who is dominant right: this must be rectified by remedial training.

Problems of rectitude.

the right hip joint and thus placing more weight onto the right shoulder, thereby compounding the difficulty for the horse of stretching into the right rein.

This overloading of the right lateral also explains why horses break down more on their right sides, and why they canter better to the left and tend to shy and run out at fences to the left. To overcome this fault of rectitude, the rider must ride forward with impulsion and engage the horse's head and neck to bring up the withers, round off the back and engage the hind legs — that is, to put the horse on the axis of the 'power curve'.

It must be noted that man also has symmetric faults similar to horses: in most cases our left side is weaker; we cross our left leg more easily than our right; we can bend our legs more easily to the left; we can turn our heads more easily to the left than right. Naturally our faults of symmetric imperfection superimpose upon those of the horse.

CHAPTER 6

Lateral Flexibility

Riding Circles, Curves and Spirals

The purpose of these exercises is to start remedying the incurvature of the horse's body by inflexion on circles, by strengthening and suppling the relevant muscles: longissimus dorsi, psoas minor and major, iliacus, tensor fasciae latae, gluteus medius, biceps and quadriceps femoris. On the circle, each lateral is exercised alternatively, to the inside of the circle in flexion and to the outside in extension. During each diagonal movement, the extension of the shoulder on the outside associates itself with the flexion of the inside hind leg. By the continual development of this action, we gradually obtain lateral suppleness and prepare the horse for lateral work on three and four tracks.

Shoulder-In, Travers, Renvers, Half- and Full Passes

The purpose of these exercises is to continue towards obtaining complete straightness of the horse's body, and to continue to strengthen and supple the muscles mentioned above. They also build up the shoulder muscles: the brachiocephalicus, supraspinatus, infraspinatus, teres major, pectoral, deltoid and

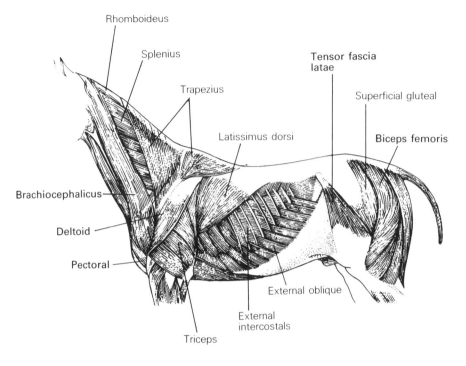

i) Superficial muscles

Equine musculature effecting lateral flexibility.

coracobrachialis, and strengthen the leg muscles: extensors, adducters, flexors and abductors.

With the above exercises, we thus obtain the maximum strength, lengthening, oscillation, and engagement of the hind legs (suppleness). It is the degree of engagement and trigger release of the three joints of the hind leg that determines elevation (collection) and lengthening (extension) of all the gaits and all movements derived from them. The more the hind legs are engaged near the line of maximum thrust, the more their propulsion exerts backward force. Because of the diagonal rhythm during the time of suspension, and transfer of weight from one diagonal to the other, the horse is robbed of the complete crossing of his legs because the leg being crossed disengages itself a fraction of a second prematurely. The more the hind legs are drawn back to the line of maximum lift, the more force is exerted upward. The degree of elevation during the suspension phase

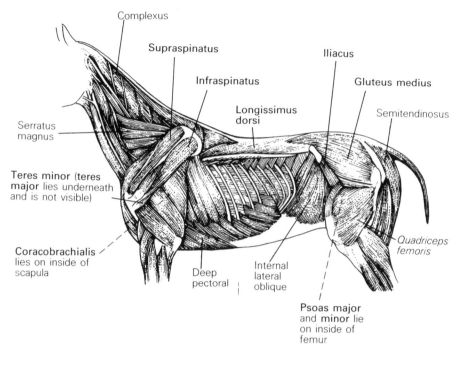

ii) Deep muscles

also depends on the strength of the hindquarters and degree of compression (extensor − flexor muscles). It is precisely at the moment the hind leg passes the vertical on its path from rear to front that compression and the closing of the angles of the articulations are at their maximum.

Half- and Full Passes, Zigzags, Counter Changes of Hand

In addition to their other function, half- and full passes, together with these other exercises, help develop the roundness and expression of the trot. For example, in crossing the forelegs, the outside foreleg must, more than on a straight line or on a circle, elevate at knee and shoulder to avoid hitting the inside foreleg while crossing over. The outside hind leg must also round off its gesture and reach more forward for the same reason. In the canter, the horse jumps from one lateral to another, thus avoiding any crossing of his legs, as we will see later when discussing half-passes. Only in the walk can a horse obtain total lateral engagement of his legs. Lateral work is thus responsible for muscular development, suppleness, collection, extension, balance to some degree, cadence, agility and ease of movement and, most of all, straightness.

CHAPTER 7

⸺○⸺

Riding Conduction on a Straight Line

⸺○⸺

NO MATTER HOW SUPPLE WE MAKE A HORSE laterally and longitudinally during training, we are constantly realigning his narrower shoulders with his wider haunches. To make the horse straight, the right and left haunches must follow the right and left shoulders respectively on two parallel tracks in the direction taken. To have a straight horse, the rider must be straight; equal weight on both seat bones, hands together, reins at equal length, shoulders at the same height, head up, sight straight ahead. Sight is very important to the rider. As when riding a bicycle, if the rider looks right, he or she will sub-consciously bring body weight to the right side and will auto-matically turn right, (and vice versa to the left).

The horse must be supple longitudinally and laterally. The more the rider collects, the more he or she must ride in shoulder-fore, to prevent the inside hind leg from slipping the haunches to the inside of the track. This is also true for transitions and canter departs. A good simple method to make a young horse straight, is to change diagonals at the rising trot every four, three, and two strides in sequence. This is especially efficacious cross-country. The exercise builds up the weak diagonal and develops cadence in the early stages of training. A horse who is constantly trotted on the same diagonal will tend to canter on the same lead. He will become crooked and will use himself much more on one side than the other. To trot, a horse associates his legs by

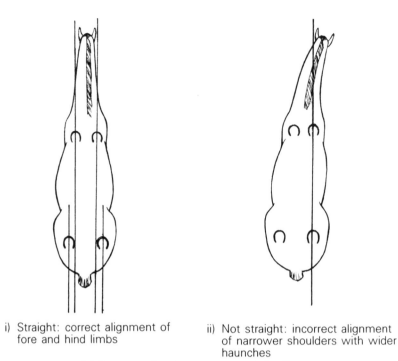

i) Straight: correct alignment of
   fore and hind limbs

ii) Not straight: incorrect alignment
    of narrower shoulders with wider
    haunches

Riding conduction on a straight line.

diagonal pairs. The diagonal takes the name of the foreleg; right
diagonal signifying right foreleg with left hind leg. A diagonal is
supported when its legs are on the ground and is suspended
when its legs are in the air. A rider trots on the right diagonal
when his or her buttocks contact the saddle as the right foreleg
touches the ground. The weak diagonal is always the one which
feels more uncomfortable to rise on. There is, therefore, an
incentive to rise more on the weak diagonal to make it stronger.

CHAPTER 8

⌐⊖¬

The Musculature of the Horse Related to Training

⌐⊖¬

M USCLES HAVE THREE PROPERTIES: contractibility, elasticity and tonicity.

CONTRACTIBILITY is the property of a muscle which produces shortening. A muscle can contract to a third of its length at rest. ELASTICITY is the property which allows the muscle to lengthen. TONICITY is the tension that resides continually in living muscle tissue. Even when a horse is in a state of rest, many muscles remain in some degree of permanent tension, if the distances that separate their parts of attachment are superior to their normal length. Excessive tonicity creates cramps and spasms. Reduction of tonicity creates atrophy.

Contractibility, elasticity and tonicity are developed by gymnastic training. To lengthen a muscle we have to ride on curves, to stretch the horse's outside lateral, and may ride forward on straight lines in the working and extended gaits in a slightly lengthened frame. To shorten a muscle, we must ride on curves to flex the muscles of the inside lateral, and in collected gaits with a shortened frame.

Muscles are also divided into two categories: quick twitch and slow twitch. The former contract and relax rapidly, while the latter contract and relax slowly. The development of these muscles depends upon conformation, heredity, and the activity of the endocrine glands. Horses with a majority of quick twitch muscles have talent for speed and endurance, since these muscles are relatively long in form and are better able to disperse lactic acid. A properly-conditioned racehorse has long sleek muscles. Horses with an abundance of slow twitch muscles have talent for lift and high-level dressage; since their muscles are relatively short in length and bulky. A properly trained Grand Prix horse will have this type of muscles, especially on his thighs, and in the gluteal group on the haunches. We cannot say that any one breed of horse will have quick twitch or slow twitch muscles only; what we do know is that it is always best to select a horse with the type of muscles needed to suit his ultimate use. This is another reason why heredity and genetics are so important an aspect in buying a young horse. Horses with a preponderance of either category of muscle can be trained to a certain level of development, but only those who are suited to their ultimate goal will progress further in training without problems, and achieve greatness.

Muscles must also function as bracing agents. For instance, muscles act together to brace the horse's vertebral column in order to allow the muscles that propel the haunches and shoulders to find a solid base of support to exert maximum effective thrust and optimum effort. Without tension, one can have force, but one cannot have propulsion.

Muscles also have to act as shock absorbers. For instance, when a jumping horse lands on a foreleg, the whole weight of his body is on that leg for a moment. The extensor and flexor muscles that were responsible for lift now fill with tension to prevent any excessive movement of the joints of the supporting leg.

What we must understand is that almost every muscle in the horse's body has a congener muscle. For instance, when a muscle contracts to produce incurvation of the neck, its congener muscle will resist by contracting itself, giving only the amount of flexion required, and in turn will produce a straightening, or reverse movement. When two congener muscles act simultaneously (vertical movement), it is their antagonist muscles that fill the role of support. A muscle can contract with maximum efficiency when the elasticity of its congener is more developed.

When we train a young horse, we should always start work in elongation, because resistance can only be destroyed by developing elasticity of the muscles. Once the muscles are supple, we can develop contractibility and tonicity. With these facts in mind, we must remember that a horse's dominant side is stronger, convex, and more developed, and before we can undertake the strengthening of the weak concave side, we must first stretch all the congener muscles of this dominant lateral in order to have enough flexibility to flex and build the muscles of the opposing weak lateral.

Finally, we must be aware that all the muscles designed for locomotion must maintain tension in order to develop propulsion. As previously stated, we must always be careful not to overstress the horse's system by asking him to perform beyond his physical development or capability. When long periods of tension are asked of the muscles, there will be an adverse effect. The blood and lymph circulation in these muscles and the muscle fibres will not absorb the nutrients and oxygen needed for the proper development of the muscles. Too much tension will cause a build-up of lactic acid in these muscles and produce pain. This continued overstressing of the horse's body will eventually break him down physically as well as mentally.

CHAPTER 9

—❦—

Impulsion

—❦—

A HORSE'S IMPULSION HAS THREE DISTINCT QUALITIES: instinctive, mechanical and transmitted. All three qualities are needed for the desired end result.

Instinctive

—❦—

Instinctive energy is the most important of the three properties, for it is inherited, and is the very root of force. Horses are hybrids; a cross of different pure breeds. Their inherited characteristics are dependent upon evolutionary laws, which, as expounded by Abbot Mandel, state that biological characters are inherited not only from the parents, but also from a number of different ancestors, both male and female. The horse's energy, however, is inherited by 'direct line' from the sire and dam.

Federico Tesio, the very successful Italian breeder, made several interesting observations on the Thoroughbred's levels of energy, which can be applied to all breeds. Tesio's study of breeding records and statistics were compiled from the *Racing Calendar* and *Stud Book* records from 1780 to 1939, which revealed that:

> Famous racing mares are frequently poor producers for the very reasons which made them famous: they have expended so much of their nervous energy in their races that they have little left to

pass on to their progeny. This is especially true during their first period as brood mares.

Stallions who have raced until the age of six and have undergone stiff training, seldom produce good offspring when they first embark on their new career. They too have used up too much of their vitality in racing and need time and rest to restore it.

A large number of horses conventionally qualified as big distance runners come from mares who either have never raced at all, or have raced seldom or only over short distances. These mares were thus able to conserve – and therefore accumulate – their nervous energy.

The offspring of the stallions, and especially of the mares, whose careers on the race track have been long and strenuous, are frequently handsome, well developed individuals without visible flaws, but they seldom win races and are beaten by others less perfect in conformation, because they have inherited a weak dose of nervous energy from a depleted parent. These offspring, by running more slowly, will not wear themselves out and may build up a new charge of energy to pass on to their own progeny.

Tesio further believed that inherited energy came from the sex act itself. His reasoning was that, when nature produces a true love match between a stallion and a mare, very high levels of energy are produced during copulation, and from such matings great champions have been born.

Tesio's study of artificial insemination using fresh semen led him to conclude that:

Thoroughbreds resulting from artificial insemination are to all outward appearances indistinguishable from those bred naturally. They inherit the Mendelian characters in the normal way and provide a good average of handsome and well bred animals.... In the past twenty years (up to 1958) no Thoroughbred born as a result of artificial insemination has ever succeeded in winning a classic, or perhaps even a semi-classic race, in any country of the world, although almost invariably bred from outstanding parents. If even a single one had achieved a reasonable success, those in favour of artificial insemination would have proclaimed it through loudspeakers. Instead silence.

Tesio further states that 'artificial insemination applied to animals is merely a copy of the method of fertilization intended by nature for plants... a lower order of life'.

Since there was very little doping (which could hinder horses careers at stud) on the racecourses of Europe in the years of his studies and observation, we must conclude that he has made some very important points.

I have had no experience with fresh semen. I have, however, had extensive experience with frozen semen. The semen that we collected with American Breeders Services was taken from stallions during their off-season, during the cold months of late autumn and early winter. The stallions were in very light work, and well rested. During cold weather their semen is free of gel, which helps in the freezing process. Among the good freezers, I have always observed very high motility in the semen prior to freezing. Among the foals I have raised from frozen semen, and later trained, some have had more energy than others, but they were not all depleted of energy. Obviously greater numbers are needed to obtain statistics from which a conclusion can be drawn. What is apparent is that we have to know a lot about the sire and dam of a young prospect, and no amount of inherited nervous energy will be too much for competition at the highest levels.

Mechanical

Mechanical impulsion relies directly upon instinctive energy for its development. It is instinctive energy which sets in motion the muscles, stimulates their action, and is the source of the horse's mental capacity which can be lively or dull according to the amounts of energy present in his central nervous system. However, mechanical impulsion will be enhanced by the further development of the horse's body through gymnastic training. The development and strengthening of the muscles (both flexors and extensors) and ligaments, will allow increased elasticity, contractibility, and tonicity to absorb kinetic energy. In *Webster's Dictionary* kinetic energy is defined as:

> The capacity to perform work. A particle, or a piece of matter may have energy owing to two causes, its motion, or its position with reference to other particles, or pieces of matter. That owing to its motion is called actual or kinetic energy. Its numerical value is the product of one half of its mass by the square of its velocity.

Kinetic energy is produced when the horse's legs strike the ground; the impact of the hooves creating energy which is transmitted to the muscles and absorbed as potential energy of displacement. This energy reappears as kinetic energy during the second half of the stride where it imparts forward momentum to the horse's body. A horse who is on the bit, that is, in the proper frame and balance to meet the challenge being asked of him, will be able to make use of this energy by enclosing it within his muscular system, where it works in elastic tension as the muscles contract and expand to their normal length. The amount of contraction (force) exhibited by a muscle is proportionate to the degree of stimulation given by its nerves. As we have seen, some nervous systems have more energy to impart than others.

Transmitted

Transmitted impulsion is given to the horse by the rider. This form of impulsion, in essence, encloses the great ring of muscles from the horse's haunches to his jaw, through which a continuous elastic flow of energy circulates and remains at instantaneous command between the rider's legs and hands. The rider's driving aids will release this energy forward from the main muscles of locomotion in the hindquarters, (namely the gluteal muscles of the croup, the flexors of the loins, and the ilio-psoas group) to emerge in the horse's jaw which is controlled by the rider's hands. Here again we enter the domain of equestrian tact: the rider's seat, feel, and coordination of legs and hands will determine the proper use of this force. The rider's legs will create the forward force desired, which will instantaneously be controlled by the hands which, through delicate feel, can release this force into forward thrust, or resist the forward force as much as necessary to create a shortening of the horse's frame via upward thrust.

It is safe to conclude that a dull, lethargic horse can be made to go forward with strong rider aids, but will never attain greatness in any equestrian sport. Such horses must find homes with Sunday riders who wish quiet contentment on a lower scale of activity.

CHAPTER 10

─o─

Tempo, Cadence, Rhythm and Self-Carriage

─o─

R HYTHM IS THE REGULARITY OF FOOTFALL, OR PERIOD of foot-fall. In the walk 1−2−3−4, in the trot 1−2, in the canter 1−2−3. Every horse has a different rhythm but this must not be too slow or too hurried. When a horse finds his natural rhythm, he will also show relaxation. When rhythm is stabilized, the rider can increase or decrease the tempo.

TEMPO is rated speed measured in metres per minute (across ground).

CADENCE is rhythm plus impulsion. It results from the proper development of extensor and flexor muscles. Cadence is the mother of collection and extension; it is the purest expression of rhythm.

SELF-CARRIAGE. What impression does a horse give a rider when he erects himself in self-carriage? The most pleasant a rider can feel... a sensation of complete lightness to the hands, perfect balance, and great propulsive power of the hindquarters. The rider is complete master of a horse who, through long and arduous training, has regained under saddle the spirit and athleti-cism he first enjoyed at play in the freedom of open land. To the rider, equine self-carriage has, throughout the ages proven to be a drug, and many strong men have become addicted.

CHAPTER 11

The Walk

THE WALK IS A TRANSVERSE LATERAL GAIT WITH FOUR distinct beats, the rhythm of which is: left hind – left fore – right hind – right fore; or alternatively starting with the right hind. In competition we are asked to present the walk in different degrees of collection. The three walks we are most concerned with are collected, medium and extended.

In the collected walk, the horse erects himself in a shortened frame in self-carriage by shifting weight to his hindquarters, and swinging his hind legs forward to strike just short of the hoof prints of his forelegs.

In the medium walk, the horse's frame is only slightly collected, weight being evenly distributed between the haunches and shoulders. The hind legs swing forward to strike in the hoof prints of the forelegs.

In the extended walk, the horse lengthens his frame, reaching somewhat down into the bit and shifting more weight to his shoulders. His hind legs swing forward to their maximum, striking as much in front of the hoofprints of the forelegs as possible.

If the horse's walk is naturally bad, training, no matter how good, will never make it great. A great natural walk can, however, be ruined by bad training. To understand the walk we must examine the key elements which are suppleness, strength, the degree of collection, mechanical impulsion and tempo.

Suppleness and strength are self-explanatory. It is obvious

that a young or untrained horse will not have the physical qualities needed to erect himself in self-carriage to perform a correct collected walk, the degree of engagement being entirely dependent upon the physical development of the horse.

Mechanical impulsion is energy created by the horse's footfalls against the ground. When one of the limbs strikes the ground, it produces kinetic energy, which is stored in the muscles of the leg and becomes potential energy of displacement. It then reappears in the second half of the stride of that leg as kinetic energy, imparting forward thrust. In the walk, the concussions of the feet against the ground are much less than in the trot and canter, therefore smaller amounts of energy can be created. Also, since the young or untrained horse's musculature is under-developed, the only means left for him to help himself forward is by using his neck as a fulcrum. If the rider restricts the horse's free use of his neck at this stage, the walk will soon become stiff, irregular, and short. This is one of the reasons why the horse must not be collected in the walk until he is very advanced in his training.

Tempo is the next most important factor. The more a horse is urged forward in increased tempo, or in lengthening, the more the diagonal support tends to become a lateral support, the lower the footfalls to the ground, and, when pushed to the extreme, the walk will become completely lateral, or a two-beat amble: right hind and right fore − left hind and left fore.

La Guérinière wrote: 'The utility of the walk is the necessity of the trot.' How right he was! But in view of the above how can we use the walk to our advantage in training without initially ruining the gait? The answer is simple: very little kinetic energy is produced by the horse's footfalls against the ground in the walk and muscle tension is minimal. The back muscles do not have to contract to brace the vertebral column to absorb the lesser upward thrust against it in the walk. The horse is, therefore, freer of tension and more able to learn obedience to the rider's aids, and the basic lateral and longitudinal exercises needed later in the trot and canter. It might be argued that this walk training will take us back to square one, and we will spoil the horse's walk but this is not so. In training the horse to obey the rider's aids in lateral and longitudinal exercises in the walk, you simply maintain minimal contact, do not collect, and keep the horse in shoulder-fore and shoulder-in. In lateral bend you can maintain the diagonal base of support and prevent any lateral tendencies the horse may try to develop.

A horse who is born with a true two-beat amble will be impossible to correct completely. It will, however, be possible to produce some improvement of the gait. Over the years I have found three methods that have helped:

1) Constant walk work on a steep long incline of say 45 degrees.
2) Always riding the walk in shoulder-in.
3) Slowing down the tempo.

A horse born with a normal walk will show great improvement in that gait, providing his training is sound and classical, while a horse with a great walk will not lose the brilliance of the gait if his training remains sound.

The medium and extended walks fall into the same category of training. The rider must always be careful not to override these gaits for fear of disrupting the diagonal base of support and shortening the strides. The rider must always maintain relaxation, rhythm, and the free forward oscillation of the hind legs. So many bad walks are observed in International Competition today that the F.E.I. has encouraged riders to ride the extended walk on a longer rein than in the past and they even allow competitors to hand-ride this movement (urge the horse forward with the hands) to develop as much overtracking as possible!

Great walks are not made, they are created by a Greater Power. When you encounter one, savour it... when you inherit a bad walk, slow it down in shoulder-in, and go to the hills! Perhaps you will not have to hand-ride your mount when crossing an important diagonal in mid-competition.

CHAPTER 12

⌐○¬

The Trot

⌐○¬

T HE TROT IS A DIAGONAL GAIT WITH TWO DISTINCT beats, the
rhythm relating to an alternating support of the diagonal
pairs; right hind together with left fore – period of suspension
– left hind together with right fore. The rhythm of the trot
remains the same whether the trot is collected or extended; only
the length of the stride changes. The trot is the horse's most
natural gait, and the touchstone of all training. Before the ultimate
development of collection the trot remains the least tiring of the
three natural gaits, for both hind and forelegs develop the same
amount of kinetic energy, and perform the same amount of
work.

In competition we are concerned with working and collected
trots, the lengthening of stride and medium and extended trots.
The development of the working trot is covered in the chapter
on lungeing so we will therefore proceed to examine the other
gait variants.

Collected Trot

⌐○¬

In the collected trot, the horse reaches collection and cadence
just short of the passage, gaining in height what he loses in
length. The strides must maintain perfect rhythm, cadence, and

engagement of the hocks. The engagement and flexion of the joints of the hind legs allow the haunches to lower, shifting more weight to the hindquarters, thus allowing the neck and head to raise. The poll must remain the highest point of the neck, and the head must be engaged slightly in front of the perpendicular. If the collection of the head is perpendicular or, behind it, the horse will lose impulsion, and the oscillation of the back muscles will lose optimum elasticity. A correct collected trot is the result of the utmost care in systematic training of the lateral and longitudinal exercises. The main faults observed in the collected trot are irregular steps, which are the result of improper gymnastic training or lameness, and floating 'passage' steps, which are the result of too much tension, or lack of strength, especially in the hindquarters. In the case of tension, the horse must be ridden forward to lengthen the stiff muscles. Lack of strength can be a problem − I have observed this fault from time to time in certain equine families within different breeds, where genetic inheritance produces successive generations of horses with weak hindquarters. Only extensive gymnastic work in the trot and canter, especially cross-country on hills, can improve this problem within an individual horse.

Lengthening of the Stride

This is asked for in the beginning of training before the horse has gained sufficient suppleness and strength to perform the extended trot. In lengthening the stride, the horse extends his frame, shifting weight to his forehand, reaches down with light flexion in his poll and 'chases' his bit forward: with his muscles lengthened, his back up and relaxed, the horse will cover as much ground per stride and show as much elasticity and suspension as his natural strength and cadence allow.

The lengthening of stride in the trot is the first longitudinal exercise. The transitions should be asked for out of the working trot and back into the working trot, because the horse has too much weight on his forehand to be able to move himself back into a collected gait of this stage of training.

The Medium and Extended Trots

These are developed out of high collection, total development of the musculature system, mechanical impulsion, and the ultimate expression of self-carriage. In the medium and extended trots, the horse lowers his haunches by flexion of the joints in his hind legs, and transfers his weight and centre of gravity to the rear. This allows the forehand to rise, and the forelegs to move forward in even, rounded strides that alight in the spot the tip of the front hooves point when they reach their apex during the second phase of the stride forward. The hind legs must reach to a point just short of the line of maximum thrust. The fore and hind legs must compose an outline of two compasses opened to the same degree. The only difference between the medium and extended trots is that in the extended trot there is increased flexion and thrust of the hindquarters resulting in greater elevation, impulsion and self-carriage.*

The main faults observed in the medium and extended trots are:

1) The hind legs lack engagement and forward thrust, and are often accompanied by a stiff flipping action of the horse's forelegs. This fault is caused by weak hindquarters, which, as we have seen, can come from lack of gymnastic development or genetic inheritance. The flipping of the forelegs can also be caused by too much tension − riding more forward can help alleviate this.

2) The hind legs step wide of the tracks of the forelegs and the horse transfers weight to his forehand. This fault results from a flaw in conformation; hind legs either set too wide, or bowed. Although very little can be done to correct this fault, I have had varying success by riding the medium and extended trots on large circles, and bending the horse as much as possible in shoulder-in while on the circle riding half-halts with an upward hand action, to keep the horse from overloading his shoulders. If the hind legs are stepping wide through lack of suppleness and strength, it is probably because the horse is not yet ready for the extended trot.
*See Notes

Medium trot.

Extended trot.

3) The horse becomes too low in the neck and behind the bit, in which case impulsion will be dissipated and maximum expression of the gait lost. In the medium and extended trot the poll must remain the highest point, with the head carried slightly in front of the perpendicular to allow the impulsion to flow through the horse's body.

4) Irregular steps. This fault is usually caused by stiffness or weakness in the hindquarters, in which case it is back to the basic lateral exercises in the working trot. If the irregularity persists, a veterinarian should be consulted to check for physical problems.

5) Loss of balance. This fault can be caused by any of the foregoing problems, uneven footing, or a momentary lapse of the horse's proprioceptive sense.

6) Disguising the medium trot. International judges have always wanted to see the medium trot ridden forward just under the demands of the extended trot. This tends to make a rider whose horse possesses an average-to-poor trot ride the medium at the same rate as the extended. This tactic rarely succeeds, since a knowledgeable judge will want to see a distinction between the two extensions. A good mark might be given for the so-called medium, but when the extended follows, the mark will have to be 'insufficient'.

The training of the medium and extended trots should not be started before the third phase of training. If asked for too soon, the trot in general can be ruined.

Great emphasis has been placed on the medium and extended trots during the modern history of academic equitation, primarily because these gaits represent the cumulative efforts of proper gymnastic training and the utmost development of suppleness, strength, balance and impulsion. In just about every National and F.E.I. test, one of the first movements called for is a medium, or extended, trot across a diagonal. This creates a very important first impression on the judge or judges; furthermore, this first extension is always followed by at least two others during the tests, which, to my mind, perhaps places too much emphasis on trot extensions, and unduly favours the horse with a great trot, especially at the lower levels of competition.

CHAPTER 13

The Canter

THE HORSE'S CANTER IS A TRANSVERSE GAIT, AS opposed to the leaping gait of a cheetah. It has three beats, the rhythm of which is (for the right lead): left hind (first beat), right hind and left fore together (second beat), right fore (third beat), followed by a period of suspension when all four legs are off the ground.

Many horsemen feel that the true collected canter has a four-beat rhythm, the fourth beat occurring when a hind leg strikes the ground before the corresponding diagonal foreleg. This timing is not visible to the naked eye unless it becomes very pronounced and is accompanied by loss of impulsion and elevation. When this occurs, the canter becomes a deficient four-beat gait and a severe fault in classical dressage.

The racing gallop is very visibly four-beat. As speed increases, the horse's vertebral column braces in order to absorb the great forces imparted by the limbs striking against the ground, the spine, thus somewhat straightened, allows the horse's feet to travel forward on straight lines — the hind legs contacting the ground visibly before their corresponding diagonal forelegs. It might be said, therefore, that the timing of footfall changes toward four-beat as the canter is highly collected, or lengthened into a gallop. In competition we must only think of three clear audible beats in the collected, medium, extended and counter-canters. Before further discussion, it is necessary to understand some of the difficulties that arise in developing the canter.

Of the three gaits, the canter is the most difficult for the horse to find his balance under the rider, the fundamental problems being the horse's rectitude the stiffness in his hind legs. Let us examine the problems of a horse who is dominant right. This horse will be convex on his right lateral, and concave on his left lateral. When, during the first phase of training we ask this horse to canter on his left lead, we will observe that the horse's concavity places his haunches to the left (inside) and, because of stiffness in his strong right hind, he transfers his croup even farther to the inside. We are therefore confronted with two problems; one of inflexion from a problem of rectitude, and one of deviation from a strong, stiff right hind. Cantering on the right lead, however, will not pose such a problem because the horse's right lateral is convex, and the thrusts from his left hind are weaker. Therefore, we will not observe as much inflexion and deviation to the right (inside). However, it is not *necessarily* the case that horses will canter better on their right leads if they are dominant right; on the contrary, if their right hind legs are *not* stiff through over-development, they will tend to canter better on their left leads, because their outside hind (right) legs are stronger than their inside hind (left) legs. In the canter it is the outside hind leg that carries the majority of the weight.

Canter training should not start until the end of the first phase of training, or indeed, until the horse is supple, strong and balanced in the trot. If 'the utility of the walk is the necessity of the trot', then 'the quality of the trot is reflected in the canter!'

Since the rectitude and gymnastic development of the horse will be discussed in future chapters, I will proceed to describe the different canters and the problems that can arise.

The Collected Canter

In the collected canter, the thorax rises in its sling to bring up the horse's back, weight is shifted to the rear, the haunches lower by virtue of increased flexion of the joints of the hind legs, the neck rises out of the shoulders in an elegant arc, the poll remains at the highest point, and the head is flexed almost to the perpendicular. The horse covers ground in soft, energetic strides that maintain a perfect three-beat rhythm, engaging his hind legs just in front of the line of maximum lift. The horse must give the impression that he is ready to extend at the slightest suggestion.

The Medium Canter

In the medium canter, the thorax lowers somewhat in its sling, weight is evenly distributed between the haunches and shoulders, the neck lowers and reaches somewhat forward, the poll remains the highest point, and the head is flexed as in collected canter. The horse covers more ground in energetic strides that maintain their three-beat rhythm, the hind legs engaging to a point just behind the line of maximum thrust. The horse remains united, on the bit, and gives the impression that he can return to the collected canter at the slightest suggestion. The medium canter must be ridden just short of the extended canter.

The Extended Canter

In the extended canter, the thorax lowers completely in its sling and transfers more weight to the horse's forehand, the neck lowers and reaches a fraction more forward than in the medium canter, the head remains flexed at 45 degrees at the poll. The hind legs engage to the line of maximum thrust and the horse covers as much ground as possible in lower, longer and impulsive strides. The horse must give the impression that he is completely relaxed and under control, in spite of the greater forward thrust. The rhythm may tend to become four-beat, but it will not be noticeable to the naked eye.

Medium canter.

Extended canter.

The Counter-Canter

The counter-canter serves three purposes: to straighten a horse, to promote flexion of the joints of the outside leg and to indicate to dressage judges the extent and quality of the horse's lateral suppleness. A horse who is dominant right and concave on his left lateral can be made straighter in the canter by counter-cantering to the right rein, in left lead down the long sides of the riding hall — the short sides having to be ridden a little wider than normal when beginning this training. Eventually the horse should be made to counter-canter on wide circles to the right and left. On a circle in the counter-canter, a horse cannot be bent along the line of the circumference; he has to remain slightly bent around the rider's inside leg, and thus bent, he follows the curvature of the circle. Constant even bend must be maintained, and the haunches must not be allowed to drift to the rider's inside. Most of all, it is imperative to maintain rhythm, tempo and impulsion. I hesitate to say that the counter-canter is a suppling exercise for in reality, true suppleness can only be achieved in the trot. The counter-canter is, however, a very useful exercise to develop flexion and thrust of the horse's outside hind leg, which is so important to canter work. Finally, the counter-canter is used in competition to evaluate the horse's fundamental gymnastic training, since lack of lateral suppleness will become very apparent in the counter-canter movements.*

Faults in the Canter

The main faults most often observed in the canter are:

1) Four-beat rhythm. This fault can originate from poor rectitude, stiffness, and lack of strength in the hindquarters and back. As previously stated, only further gymnastic work in the trot can improve the situation. Horses that persist in cantering in four beats, after extensive gymnastic training in

*See Notes

the trot, will never overcome this fault altogether. I have had some success in reconstructing the canter stride and balance by repeated canter departs on a wide circle. I make the horse responsive and extremely sensitive to my inside leg in order to develop as much thrust as possible from the horse's hind legs. I place the horse on a 15 metre circle, and ensure that the figure is absolutely round. From the collected walk in shoulder-fore, I strike off and canter four strides in shoulder-fore then ride a transition to walk four strides in shoulder-fore then strike off into canter and repeat. After several canter departs in one direction, I ask for a half pirouette in the walk, and immediately strike off out of the last stride of the pirouette in the canter on the new lead, and repeat the transitions and walk strides in the new direction. As the canter strides gain in elevation and thrust, I increase their number and reduce the number of walk strides. When the horse can canter several revolutions correctly, I ask for counter-canter on the circle, interrupted by walk strides and half pirouettes in the walk to establish a new direction and canter lead. The secret of success in this work is to make the horse exceptionally responsive to your inside leg, to demand increased thrust from the horse's hind legs (outside − inside in that order) and to make the transitions in perfect rhythm.

2) Horses who show a faster tempo on one lead than the other. This fault is always a fault of rectitude and can best be corrected on circles. Let us assume that we are dealing with a horse who is dominant right and the rhythm of his canter stride is faster on the left lead. To correct this problem I place the horse on a large circle to the right and ride a lively working canter on the right lead, after which I counter-canter this circle on the left lead to develop maximum thrust from the right hind leg.

3) Horses who canter wide behind. This problem is often observed in stallions, or in horses who are built wide behind, or are outright bow-legged. These horses disengage their hind legs, raise their croups, transfer weight to their fore-hands, fall out of balance, and in extreme cases use the rider's hands as a 'fifth leg'. Such horses have to be ridden on 8 metre circles, and voltes of 6 metres. They must not be

allowed to lose rhythm or impulsion on the circles. When cantering on straight lines, they must be kept constantly in shoulder-in. I have used renvers and travers canters from time to time with such horses, but I have always found that shoulder-in is best, for it allows complete control over the inside hind leg, and helps in regaining engagement, balance and straightness.

4) Horses who disengage the inside hind leg. This is a common problem, especially among young horses. A horse with this tendency swings his inside hind over so slightly to the outside of the track of the foreleg of the same side. This fault is easily overcome by keeping the horse in shoulder-fore until the lateral is properly realigned.

5) Haunches falling to the inside. This has to be the most common fault observed in competition, especially in the medium and extended canters, and their transitions back to the collected canter. The best way to correct this fault is to practise the extensions in shoulder-in, and to increase the bend going into the transitions to collected canter. The rider must use the direct, or lateral half-halt to be most effective. These extensions must also be ridden down the long sides in the counter-canter allowing the wall to restrain the horse's haunches from falling in. The fly in the ointment is the lengthening on the diagonal with transition at the corner letter. Almost every horse has a tendency to flatten his haunches to the outside in anticipation of regaining the track. The best way to correct this fault is to use a diagonal half-halt one stride in front of the marker, maintaining re-straining contact with both legs slightly further back on the horse's flanks than normal, and then counter-canter the corner. When the transition at the marker is straight and smooth and without any deviation of the haunches, then the flying change should be introduced. The flying change must be asked for simultaneously with the transition one horse's length in front of the marker, so that the rider's knee and shoulder are parallel to the marker as the new canter lead is established. There is no fault more glaring, or worse than a wishy-washy transition with haunches flattening to the outside, followed by a flip-flop out of balance in the corner.

Later on in training, the development of the piaffe in hand and ridden will automatically improve the canter. The further gymnastic development and increased flexion of the hind legs greatly helps the canter stride.

The main rider errors in the canter are failure to obtain response to the inside leg, and not giving with the fingers on the reins at the end of the third beat before the time of suspension. The horse must not be restrained at this moment; he must be free to jump forward.

If you have any question about the finished quality of a horse's canter, put him on a figure of eight with loops of 10 metres and canter the figure, reins in one hand, right and left, without flying changes...

CHAPTER 14

My Progression

E VERY HORSE IS DIFFERENT, AND THAT IS WHAT MAKES training interesting. Before training can be undertaken, we must analyse each horse in detail. A careful study of his conformation will give clues to physical weaknesses and strengths. We must be familiar with the animal's eating, drinking, and sleeping patterns, for these will give us an idea of the horse's stable manners, and powers of recuperation. We must have an exact knowledge of his rectitude, balance, gaits and athletic ability. Last, but not least, we must understand the horse's character; only then can we devise a training schedule best suited to his needs, and set sail for the ultimate goal, whatever it might be.

In my own case, the impact of these factors is that, while my basic method never varies, its application may, because I keep an open mind and remain receptive to any new knowledge a horse may impart, and am willing to adapt my programme to resolve or circumvent any particular problems encountered.

Bearing this in mind, the following outline is my suggested guideline for the development of a young horse all the way to the highest levels of competition.

First Phase: Foundation of lateral and longitudinal flexibility

LUNGEING
Development of the overall muscular system.
Producing rhythm and relaxation.
Suppling hindquarters.
Putting horse on bit (side reins).
Cavalletti work.
Small jumps.

RIDDEN
Cross-country work.
Rising trot, changing diagonals every 4−3−2 strides in low head carriage.
Establishing rhythm.
Jumping small natural obstacles in the trot.
Turn on the forehand to teach obedience to inside and outside leg.
Riding large circles, half circles, reverse half circles, centre line, across diagonals in working trot.
Canter on 20 metre circles, changing rein across diagonals with single changes through the trot at the short sides and at X.
Lengthening stride in trot.
Developing half-halts.

CHECK POINTS
Horse must be very sensitive to rider's aids.
Balanced, forward, and straight in working trot.
Becoming more comfortable to rise on weak diagonal.
Horse relaxed and calm.

Second Phase: Developing the strength to carry

WORK IN HAND
Start piaffe training (half steps forward).

RIDDEN
Shoulder-fore.
Shoulder-in.
Travers — Renvers.
Half-passes and full passes in the trot starting and finishing in shoulder-fore.
Counter changes of hand, and zigzags in the trot.
Transitions trot — walk — trot.
Full halt from the trot.
Rein-back.
Turn on the haunches out of shoulder-fore.
All school figures in the trot.
Canter departs along the wall right, left, right.
Simple changes through the walk.
Half-passes in canter from centre line to track, and from track to centre line (starting in shoulder-fore), with simple changes at the wall.
Counter-canter.
Full halt from the canter — rein-back then canter on, left and right leads.
All transitions trot and canter.
Single flying change, left and right leads.

CHECK POINTS
Hindquarters supple.
Back muscles relaxed.
Forehand light.
Neck arched according to degree of collection, and steady.
Ears on level plane.
Geometric bend even on both laterals.
Rectitude and balance.

Third Phase: Collection, extension and self-carriage

EXERCISES

Collected walk – extended walk.

Collected trot – extended trot.

Collected canter (up to canter on the spot), extended canter.

All transitions.

Piaffe.

Passage.

Flying changes every four, three, two and one stride.

Zigzags in the canter.

Working pirouettes and pirouettes on the centre line.

Acute half-passes in the trot and canter.

CHECK POINTS

Horse forward-going, straight, light and relaxed.

In self-carriage during all transitions.

Cadence evident at all gaits.

Variations

There are a few variations from this theme that seem to recur often with many of my horses:

I will often start work in hand earlier – almost immediately toward the end of the first phase. I have found that when this work is properly introduced, it is a wonderful exercise to develop the total musculature of the horse's body, and when piaffe is trained over a long period of time with patience and great moderation, it brings out the maximum beauty and expression. All too often trainers wait too long to teach piaffe, and when they start, they ask too much too fast and end up on the chicken farm doing the 'rooster scratch'.

When the horse's canter is very good, I will introduce flying changes almost at the start of the second phase. I have found that such horses have little difficulty in learning the changes, and if taught before the horse becomes very supple, the initial flying changes will be very straight. Once the changes have been trained at this stage, I will back off until the horse becomes stronger in the third phase. If the horse's canter is weak, I will not attempt any canter work until late in the second phase when, through greater gymnastic development in the trot, the horse will have become better prepared to canter.

Horses must not be trained to become like robots through constant drilling of movements and exercises. The daily work must vary and the horse always kept fresh and attentive. As much training as possible should be done while riding cross-country. Horses trained to the highest levels by drilling and force, only become stiff, one-sided, dull performers. A horse trained to the highest level gymnastically with tact and equestrian knowledge, will become beautiful of body, alert of mind, and will show a certain something of his trainer's character. This is where sport meets art, and they merge into one.

CHAPTER 15

⌒о⌐

Lungeing

⌒о⌐

L UNGEING IS ONE OF THE MOST IMPORTANT EXERCISES in training. It is the first serious contact the trainer has with the horse, and good lungeing techniques can create a good first impression on a horse. Lungeing is a subject that has received little attention in equestrian literature and is misused and little understood by many horsemen.

The main reasons for lungeing the horse are:

1) As the first exercise in the process of training the young horse.
2) The further gymnastic development of the horse's body without the weight of the rider.
3) To teach the horse the proper acceptance of the bit.
4) To render the horse completely obedient to the voice and all work in hand.
5) For the re-training of spoiled horses.

The proper equipment needed to lunge a horse consists of:
A light lungeing cavesson.
A long narrow canvas lunge line fitted with a buckle.
Side reins.
A long lunge whip.

General Principles of Lungeing
—o—

BENEFITS OF WORKING ON A CIRCLE

The first fundamental principle is to create a perfectly round circle. This is easier said than done. On a 12 to 15 metre circle, the horse's body must be geometrically bent, allowing his inside hind leg to flex and oscillate to the medial line, to exactly the same degree at every stride, and to allow his outside hind leg to stretch to exactly the same length at each stride.

While working on this circle, the horse must be allowed to lower his neck and chase the bit downward and forward. A horse in this frame will be able to develop suppleness, strength, balance and proper acceptance of the bit. Suppleness is developed by stretching the neck, back muscles and the outside lateral. Strength is developed by flexing the inside lateral. Acceptance of the bit is created by allowing the horse to find the bit of his own accord by having to chase it downward and forward, and once he takes the bit, to chew it and release it at his own will. A horse must never be put on the bit by tightening the side reins. This would only cause the horse to work against his natural instinct, with disastrous results.

THE TRAINER'S POSTURE

In order to create a perfect circle, the trainer must maintain the proper posture and position in the centre of the circle while standing upright, yet relaxed. The lungeing arm must maintain the same position as if seated in the saddle; elbow relaxed and near the side, forearm extended with the wrist slightly flexed to the inside, and the lunge line held in all five fingers, or split between the little and fourth fingers. The lunge whip is held in the other hand and, when not in use, can be held under the arm or over the shoulder of the same side. I prefer the shoulder position, for it facilitates the turning of the body. The feet must be kept in a narrow stance and the trainer must pivot around the inside heel in the direction the horse is moving and remain absolutely on the spot. The lunge line must be kept lightly taut at all times.

VOICE COMMANDS

The voice commands given by the trainer are just as important as the action of the whip and half-halts on the lunge line. Voice aids can be made in any language and can span a large vocabulary ranging from the ridiculous to the sublime. As French is the soft language of lovers, German, with its guttural overtones, is often referred to as the language best suited to horses. Actually the only important thing here is tone, rather than actual words. Horses have a very keen sense of hearing and the trainer should always keep a low voice, and the commands short and precise, for example 'walk on'. If the horse does not respond, the command should be repeated in a higher tone, with a flick of the whip if necessary. To reward say 'good boy', with an elevated tone. The voice can always be raised when necessary to make correction, or to reward. Shouting has no place in correct training; it simply demonstrates the trainer's lack of patience and experience.

INITIAL RESISTANCES

At the start of lunge training, two major resistances are likely to occur.

When the horse is being lunged to his weak or concave side (usually the left) he will tend to pull out on the circle in an effort to transfer more of his weight to his stronger (right) side. This evasion will always start at exactly the same spot on the circle. It will therefore be easy for the trainer to anticipate this resistance and correct the horse by driving him forward with a flick of the whip just above the hock, whilst instantaneously placing a strong half-halt. This correction makes the horse engage his inside (left) hind, and encourages him to place more of his weight on the left lateral. It is important to have a lunge whip sufficiently long to enable the trainer to reach the horse's hind leg without having to move from the centre of the circle: this position will allow the trainer to keep the lunge line taut, and place a precise, strong half-halt.

When the horse is being lunged to his strong or convex side (usually the right), he will have more difficulty bending on the circle and will tend to drop his inside shoulder to the inside and swing his haunches to the outside, to avoid engaging his strong and stiff (right) hind leg. Again, this evasion will always occur at the same place, and the trainer must be ready to drive the horse forward by applying the whip just above the horse's hock to drive the horse forward and re-establish the circle. The horse should thus engage his inside hind and transfer more weight to his outside shoulder. However, if the horse persists in falling in, the trainer should exchange lunge and whip hands, and flick the whip about 4 metres in front of the horse; this action will keep the horse out on the perimeter of the circle.

When the lunge work is stopped and the horse is made to halt on the perimeter, it is very important to make the horse come to the trainer, rather than the trainer going to the horse. This approach makes the horse more aware of the trainer's unrelenting position at the centre of the circle, and it will also play a very important role later when work in hand is started.

EARLY PROGRESSION

As the horse progresses in his lunge training, he will become more supple and strong, thus improving his balance and being able to track properly in perfect bend. You can always evaluate the horse's progress by the width of the track of the circle; as he progresses in his training, the track will become narrower.

Lunge training must always start in the walk until the horse gains some understanding of what is being asked of him, then, almost immediately, the trainer will be able to start the horse in working trot. It would be a grave mistake to drive the horse forward in a tempo beyond his physical suppleness and strength, for doing so would ruin the true rhythm of the trot. It would also be a mistake to let the horse lag behind the bit; the trainer must, therefore, create and maintain the proper tempo and rhythm. The main points to watch in establishing the proper tempo are the horse's bend on the circle, the relaxation of the neck downwards, the contraction of the back muscles, and the engagement and swing of the hind legs. When all four conditions are favourable, the trainer will have established the tempo for the correct working trot. The horse is best made supple in the trot, for in this gait the muscles of the back flex and extend alternately on each side of the spine, in rhythm with the diagonal rising and transfer of balance in the gait – and this motion creates a suppling effect upon the whole body.

At a much later date, it is possible to canter the horse on the lunge to achieve further development of the back and stomach muscles. In the canter, the contractions and relaxations of the longissimus dorsi occur simultaneously on both sides of the vertebral column, and the flexion and lengthening of the muscles are greater; this action will help further strengthen a very weak back and supple a very stiff one. In some instances, horses who have serious flaws in their canter can be made to improve by cantering on the circle without the weight of the rider.

MORE ADVANCED EXERCISES

Once the horse has improved in bend, suppleness, strength and rectitude, the trainer can introduce new exercises that will further the horse's training. The most successful of these exercises are:

1) The diminishing circle. The trainer simply brings the horse gradually in on smaller and smaller circles until the horse can no longer turn and trot in rhythm, then the horse is let out gradually until he reaches the original perimeter.

2) Leaving one circle in lengthening the stride, back on a new circle. There the trainer leaves the inside point of the first circle and jogs in a straight line for as many metres as possible before establishing a new circle.

3) All transitions – walk – trot – walk – later on in training, trot – canter – trot, and square full halts on the perimeter.

I sometimes lunge my horses on steep hills, allowing them to lengthen the stride in the trot uphill and collect themselves downhill. This lunge work must not be attempted with very young horses, and must be kept to a minimum with the older ones. When lungeing on hills, a cavesson must always be used and the trainer must not stay centered on the circle, but must accompany the horse by walking up and down the incline.

Functional Aspects of Lungeing

Now that I have painted a broad picture of the basic philosophy of lungeing, I would like to comment more directly on the functional side of the exercise.

INTRODUCING THE YOUNG HORSE TO THE LUNGE

When starting a young horse for the first time on the lunge line, a light cavesson must be adjusted over the snaffle bridle, from which the reins must be removed. The cavesson must be fitted so that it cannot turn and rub the horse's outside eye. The best way to prevent this is to tighten the throatlash. The horse must always be started to his concave side (usually the left) and the lunge line should be attached to the inner ring on the noseband. The trainer, at first positioned slightly behind the horse's inside shoulder, and holding the lunge whip low in the right hand, must walk forward with the horse until the idea of the circle is created. At this point, the trainer can slowly establish a correct stationary position at the centre of the circle. If the horse is difficult to convince, an assistant with a short lunge whip must be brought to the inside of the circle and take up a position behind the horse's haunches in order to encourage him forward. Very soon the horse will adapt himself to the circle. His stiffness, however, will not allow him to move on an even circle, therefore the trainer must move along on a small inner circle to accompany the horse until he is able to achieve the proper bend on a correct 15 metre circle. Only then can the trainer establish the proper stationary position at the centre. As soon as some degree of proficiency has been reached to the horse's concave side, the horse must be started to his convex side (usually the right); the same procedure being followed.

LUNGEING OVER GROUND POLES AND CAVALLETTI

Once the young horse can turn with ease correctly on both reins, I introduce him to work over ground poles. This consists of placing poles on the ground at approximately 1.15 metre (3.8 feet) to 1.50 metres (4.9 feet) apart, around a 15-metre (50-foot) circle. I start with one pole and build up to six. It is of the utmost importance to space the poles to match the horse's stride. The poles are properly spaced when the horse's hind feet track exactly in the middle of the poles. It is important to have a helper on hand to readjust the poles whenever the horse displaces them by negligence. The side reins must be adjusted to allow the horse to stretch, look for the ground, and chew the bit. The horse's back muscles, namely the longissimus dorsi, latissimus dorsi, and the gluteal group, must stretch and oscilate in order to gain suppleness and strength. Once the horse is confirmed in this work I introduce him to cavalletti training on the lunge.

Cavalletti must be sturdy so that they cannot be easily displaced. They should be constructed so that they can be used at three different heights: 18 centimetres (7 inches), 30.5 centimetres (1 foot), and 40.5 centimetres (1 foot 4 inches).

When I start cavalletti training I abandon the circle and use as straight a line as the length of the lunge line will permit to approach the first cavalletto. To accomplish this you have to accom-
*

USE OF SIDE REINS IN MORE ADVANCED WORK

When this basic lunge work is completed and the horse is properly broken to the rider, I abandon the lunge work and increase the ridden work cross-country. I will soon return to lungeing to impart more suppleness, strength and balance. Now, however, I will change my tactics slightly. I do away with the cavesson noseband and only return to its use for hill work or jumping. When lungeing directly off the snaffle, I use the Colbert rein attachment. This consists of passing the lunge line through the inside snaffle ring, up over the horse's poll and attaching the buckle to the outside ring. It is now time to introduce the horse to side reins. Since the horse must always be allowed to reach for the bit, it is important to adjust the side reins loosely enough to allow the horse to lower his neck and chase the bit forward, while at the same time allowing enough contact to promote slight flexion of the poll. The side reins should always be attached to the girth about 2.5 centimetres above the saddle flap, and to the snaffle rings above the reins to allow free light contact without any interference. It is important to keep both side reins at exactly the same length to maintain even contact on the horse's tongue and bars. Correct bend on the circle must come from the oscillations and suppleness of the hind legs and not by bending the horse's neck to the inside with a shortened side rein. As the horse gains more suppleness and self-carriage, the side reins will have to be shortened to accommodate the increased collection of his frame. As soon as the horse is able to lunge on a proper circle engaging his inside hind leg just in front the line of maximum thrust, while at the same time transferring weight to
*See Notes

his outside shoulder, I reintroduce him to all the other lungeing exercises such as half-halts, diminishing circles, lengthening of stride from one circle to another and so on.

Lungeing is a wonderful exercise for developing the young horse, but it can also be a dangerous one and the trainer must always be cautious not to overdo it. Too much torque on the joints and overall stress on the horse's musculature can do more harm than good. Also, horses in general become bored very quickly with this work, so a clever trainer will vary it, and constantly introduce new exercises to keep the horse keen and attentive at all times.

Retraining on the Lunge: A Personal Recollection

I cannot conclude this chapter without mentioning the benefits lungeing has in retraining a spoiled horse. One glaring example comes to my mind. Back in the early 1950's I was transferred with my family from Colombo, Ceylon (now called Sri Lanka) to Bombay, India. While my work, family, and golf consumed most of my existence, in that order, I still managed to play a little polo and participated in amateur races. I enjoyed participating in these activities, but the great heat and humidity of Asia dampened my enthusiasm for equestrian sports. My lack of interest was soon to receive a positive shock.

One day, while participating in an amateurs race meeting in Bombay, I was introduced to the Maharajah of Gwalior. During idle conversation with the Maharajah about the races, I mentioned to him my passion for dressage and jumping. The next day one of the Maharajah's aides delivered an invitation inviting me to tea with Gwalior at his estate above Breach Candy in Bombay. Tea was an excuse to have me led to his private stable where at least 200 racehorses stood in immaculate conditions, each with a *sahish* (groom) stationed in front of the stall. I was told by the aide accompanying me that the Maharajah wished me to pick any horse I wanted to train in basic dressage! Politeness dictated that

I should not spend a week trying to decide which one of these horses would be best suited for the task ahead. Using my intuition, which is usually foolishly influenced by beauty (whether of the human female or equine variety), I walked up and down the aisles until my eyes came in contact with a magnificent sculptured head, eyes bright, set apart, and a body to match all the beautiful women of India. Surely this horse would also be able to roll her hips and possess all the mechanics of the body so essential to pure gait and brilliance! So it was done, I made my choice. In all my excitement, I forgot to ask the horse's name, breeding, or age.

She was delivered to my stable at the racecourse the next day along with her *sahish*. Once a *sahish* had been assigned to a horse, it is for life. As my luck would have it, this horse turned out to be a four-year-old mare from the Nasrullah line; I regret that I do not remember her name. I could not wait to mount and experience the feel of this beautiful animal. I ask the *sahish* to saddle the mare with a Danloux jumping saddle which I used for polo, and I personally fitted her with an old Hermès snaffle bridle that was one of my treasured possessions.

No sooner had I a leg over the mare, than she took off like a Chinese rocket at New Year – violent lurches and spins all the way down the back stretch of the racecourse! Little Indian heads seemed to appear from everywhere to enjoy the massacre of the European idiot who selected such a bad horse from all the possible winners in Gwalior's stable. Being young, supple and too dumb to be scared, I eventually brought the mare back to the stable, dismounted, and asked the *sahish* to bring me a lunge line. I had no side reins, or whip, so I adjusted the snaffle reins, by tying a knot and placing them behind the pommel and under the stirrup leathers, which I left down. I ran the lunge line through the inside bit ring under the horse's chin and attached it to the outside ring for maximum contact. I lieu of a whip, I used a polo mallet.

Without further ado, or equestrian tact, I started to lunge this mare to the left and for two weeks it was a real battle of wits. I learned during this time that the mare had been ruled off the track as a rogue. After about three weeks of lunge training, she started to become docile and responsive and I was able to mount her without any disobedience, although I still lunged her five days a week before mounting.

The mare became responsive to my aids, and reached good lateral and longitudinal suppleness. I could ride correct shoulder-ins, renvers and half-passes in the trot and canter, with simple changes through the walk. Unfortunately, this experience came to a sudden end. One Saturday after riding in two races, I was taken to the hospital suffering from acute weakness. I was told that I had tropical hepatitis and would have to remain hospitalized for a month. I had Gwalior informed that I could no longer work his mare and asked if he could please take her back. This was immediately done – I heard no more about the horse.

After a long period of hospitalization I was granted six months home leave and, while in New York City I received a telegram from my racing pals in Bombay informing me that the mare won her first two starts at one mile and a quarter. With the telegram still in my hand, my mind wandered back to those early days of lunge training. Without any doubt, those lessons subdued that highly strung and confused animal. . .

'Lungeing should not be mechanical exercising, but a mental exercise in concentration of body and mind' – Gustav Steinbrecht (1808–1885).

CHAPTER 16

Starting the Young
Horse Under Saddle

THE FIRST PHASE OF TRAINING IS VERY IMPORTANT inasmuch as it is the horse's first serious encounter with man. A horse can be made, or broken, during these first weeks of work. For this reason, I proceed very slowly. I would rather be sure of my progress than sorry later on. The horses I have raised received as much attention as possible during their first two years of life. We handled them a lot, groomed them, taught them to walk correctly on the leading rein, to halt square, and to stand obediently for the farrier to trim their hooves. I have found, without exception, that warmbloods need a great deal of attention and gentle discipline during these first years, or they can grow to be quite a handful and difficult to break.

Introduction On the Lunge

When a sport horse reaches his third year, he is ready to start training. I fit the horse myself with a simple rubber snaffle and a cavesson noseband. At this stage, I do not want a drop noseband that will restrict the freedom of the jaw. I make very sure that the snaffle is properly adjusted. I then have an assistant walk the young horse around for a few days until he becomes comfortable and chews the bit softly. It is now time to introduce the horse to the lungeing cavesson, which I adjust over the snaffle, then remove the reins and attach the lunge line. I have the horse bandaged on all four legs and start lunge training. I start to the left with an assistant who walks to the inside and behind the horse with a short lunge whip. I do not stay on the spot, but walk in a large circle left to encourage the horse forward on a 20 metre circle. As the horse finds his bearings, I gradually come back on the spot to make the 20 metre circle rounder and more even. I start the same process in the trot, and as soon as the horse is able to trot on a more or less even 20 metre circle to the left, I relieve my assistant and take over all driving aids with my long lunge whip. When the horse is fairly proficient to the left, I start the same procedure to the right. When the horse is comfortable in both directions, I introduce him to the surcingle and saddle pad. It is important to tighten the surcingle progressively in order to avoid any bucking or disobedience. Once the horse accepts the surcingle and pad, it is time to introduce the saddle. When the horse accepts the saddle with the stirrups hanging loose along his flanks, and lunges calmly forward on a fairly even 20 metre circle, I bring him in to the centre of the circle and have my assistant hoist himself up slowly so that his arms are over the saddle, and repeat this exercise a few times before returning the horse to the stable.

After a few days, I have my assistant raise himself up and lay stomach-down on the saddle while I stand close by and lead them around the circle. If the horse remains calm and relaxed to this new weight in motion, the day of reckoning is close at hand. I make absolutely sure that the horse is calm, relaxed and ready before I let my assistant mount. I want to avoid, at all cost, any defence or disobedience. The horse must be confident. Every horse is different. Some can be mounted the first day; these are the ones I do not wish to own. Horses with 'blood' and character take much longer, and methodical progress and patience will pay big dividends over the long term.

Once the horse is mounted and accepts the rider's weight, I continue the lunge line training for a week or so until the horse finds his balance under the rider, turns in both directions on an even circle, learns to go forward from the rider's legs (with help from the lunge whip if necessary), and to stop when the rider raises his hands (with help from the lunge line and cavesson, if needed).

At this stage, it is time to wean the horse from the lunge line and continue basic training. In some cases when the horse is still very immature and needs more time to grow and develop, I will postpone further training, and turn the horse back out to pasture until he is ready to resume training. It is always best to break the horse early; if one waits until the fourth year, it can be much more difficult.

The basic training of a three- and four-year-old horse must remain simple and easy. I make a point of never riding three-year-olds anymore. I have found that young riders do a better job. They are free of fear, more supple, and they seem to bounce off the ground with more aptitude than old-timers!

Initial Work Under Saddle

At the start of training under saddle, I pay close attention to the horse's rectitude. If the horse is dominant right, I have my rider start in rising trot on a large circle left, rising on the left diagonal; this will help stretch the strong stiff right lateral, and at the same time strengthen the weak left lateral. After the horse has been well warmed up to the left, I have the rider go on a large circle to the right and maintain rising on the left diagonal. While still on large circles, I have the rider ask for simple transitions, such as walk to trot, trot to walk and trot, walk, halt, walk, trot. Once the young horse starts to find his balance under the rider and can perform satisfactory simple transitions, I have the rider take the horse large around the arena in rising trot, changing diagonals every four, three, two strides and back two, three, four, etc... this builds cadence and balance. The rider must make certain to ride the corners wide and in proper bend. While this work progresses, I look for the horse to start chasing his bit downward and forward. I also want to see the poll yield on light contact, and the horse chewing the bit softly.

At this stage I have the horse trot over poles on the ground, and eventually low cavalletti, adjusted to the horse's working trot stride. At this stage, I do not want to shorten or lengthen the horse's natural stride. When the horse is calm, relaxed, balanced and stretching down into the bit over the cavalletti, I have the rider trot and jump low cross-poles, and eventually low uprights and oxers; always making sure to maintain the working trot. This is a wonderful exercise for longitudinal suppleness; it brings up and exercises the shoulders, stretches the neck and arches the back.

When the horse becomes balanced under the rider in the trot work, I start asking for canter on a large circle, first to the left, if the horse is dominant right, and thereafter to the right. I do not ask the young horse to go large in the canter, but keep him on large circles until he has gained additional suppleness, strength and balance.

After this, it is time to send the horse out cross-country. At first, I only want the rider to walk on a long rein, to allow the horse to use his neck as a fulcrum to help his body forward. When the horse is calm and relaxed in the walk, I have the rider trot and change trot diagonals in sequence, after which, long rising sessions on the horse's weak diagonal. I want to see the horse trotted and jumped over all natural obstacles possible – tree trunks, small ditches; walked through shallow streams and up and down small banks. Once the young horse is well balanced in his trot cross-country, I have the rider start short canter sessions, left lead at first, then on the right lead, always on flat, even footing at first.

Progression

When the horse reaches his fourth year, basic training may become more sophisticated to include more engagement of the hindquarters and a higher degree of flexion in the poll. The horse can be introduced to all the simple school figures maintaining 10 metre arcs; lengthening and shortening of the stride in trot and canter; simple changes of lead through the trot; full halt through the walk. The horse may be taught to yield to the rider's leg by use of turns on the forehand, and if necessary, a few steps of leg-yielding on circles in the walk. I will also reintroduce lunge work in its more advanced form, to further promote suppleness and strengthening of the muscular system.

At this juncture, there are three points I would like to make clear:

1) It is important to find and establish the proper rhythm and tempo of the horse's working trot. To do this, the rider must drive the horse forward until he starts to shorten the length of his stride. This is the threshold; the point where the tempo is too fast, and the horse shortens his stride and runs forward. When you reach this threshold, back the tempo down a fraction and you will have the working trot for that particular horse. Other than to establish this threshold it is very bad practice to ride the horse forward to the point where he loses his length of stride, since this results in loss of rhythm, and eventually total loss of pure gait.

2) A young horse must never be worked to the point of physical and mental exhaustion.

3) A young horse must be punished firmly, but not brutally, for disobediences. He must be praised and rewarded for his good reactions. He must be made physically healthy and mentally happy. When a young horse shies at an object, he must not be punished. The rider must approach the object close enough to allow the horse to smell the cause of his fear, while at the same time patting him and speaking in a calming tone. The horse must never make the association that punishment follows fear, since this will compound his fearfulness.

A Cautionary Reminiscence

When I was a young boy living in Paris, I was often asked to assist in the breaking of young horses, and since this was a means to ride new horses, I was always willing and eager to oblige. I had the distinction of getting straightened out by such greats as General Albert de Carpentry and his friend, my early instructor, mentor and most ardent critic, M. Victor Laurent, and even a few horse dealers, whose names I am pleased not to remember. One such dealer had an Anglo-Norman rogue. He was a beautiful big black horse with white socks and a star — a very impressive horse and a big mover. No one had been successful in staying on him for more than a few seconds, and then with no fewer than two men hanging on to the lunge line at the same time. Day after day, the dealer brought new riders to the stable; day after day, they either departed to the hospital, or the local bistro to calm their frazzled nerves. Day after day, the dealer and his crew beat the horse to a pulp with whips. After a week of this circus, the dealer and his helpers decided to tranquilize the horse and tie down two heavy cement bags over the saddle. As soon as they gave the horse a little slack on the lunge line, he took off violently on the circle, lurching, falling down, getting up, only to start all over again. The next day, the dealer and his horse left the stable. I was never told what happened to this horse, but I didn't need much imagination to know that he had to end up on someone's dinner table! I always remember this incident, for it made me aware that horses are not born mean — men make them so. Throughout my career I have always taken extra time to break horses, not out of fear of being bucked off, but with the knowledge that if a horse is properly handled during the first months of his career, he will develop a happy, willing, and confident attitude towards his rider.

CHAPTER 17

⸻

The Full Halt

⸻

THE FULL HALT IS THE MOVEMENT MOST ASKED FOR in dressage tests, and it is surely the movement most often poorly performed. The full halt is a very important movement because it is the first impression given to the judges. The way a horse halts and the way the rider salutes gives a very good impression of what is to follow. Also, it gives a very clear indication of the suppleness of the horse's hindquarters, his balance, and degree of lightness of his forehand, his submission and the rider's use of aids and elegance.

These facts were made clear to me late one afternoon in Aachen, Germany, in 1972. I was on my way back to the stable after the close of the afternoon's jumping events. There, in the practise arena, was Joseph Neckerman on Adriano (his Olympic mount in Munich), practising halts and salutes. There was no one around the grounds, so I stood to one side of the stable door not to interrupt, or be noticed. Herr Neckerman had his wife sitting at the C marker and his groom standing at B to coach him. He must have entered, halted at X, and saluted, well over thirty times before he was satisfied. His halts were performed with such precision, suppleness, lightness and elegance that it would have been impossible to give him marks lower than nines or tens! This observation became an invaluable lesson. From that day on, I have given the training of full halts my utmost attention. It is obvious that repeatedly practising full halts will not *bring about*

The full halt.

suppleness of the hindquarters, balance, and lightness of the forehand. It will, however, promote accuracy, submission, stillness and elegance of the salute, not to mention helping proper rein-backs and transitions to canter when called for in dressage tests.

Full halts are best trained with common sense, discipline, and the proper gymnastic development of the horse's body. Common sense and discipline go hand-in-hand. First, start by ensuring that the horse is made to stand square in the stable in the cross ties, before mounting and dismounting. Cross ties are two ropes, each attached by one end to walls either side of the stable aisle, and by their other ends to the horse's halter, thus holding him centred in the aisle. When teaching the full halt ridden, I start at the walk and progress to the trot through the walk. When the horse has reached sufficient suppleness and strength to bring his hocks under to maintain self-carriage and even weight distribution, I ask for the full halts from the trot, and eventually the canter.

Full halts must always be practised at a letter in the arena, or at an object that allows the rider to halt square – the rider's knee and shoulder aligned with the marker. It is very difficult, if not impossible, for the mounted rider to know if the horse's forelegs are perfectly square. Therefore, it is best to practise full halts only when a mirror, an assistant, or a ground shadow is available.

To begin with, the full halt must be taught with very slight driving aids of legs, bracing of the lower back, and resistance of both hands. If the young horse pulls, do not pull back, simply lift the hands until the horse stops – then immediately cease all aids. As the horse progresses in training, the driving forces of the rider's legs and lower back can be increased to promote more engagement of the hocks and self-carriage, while the rider increases resistance with the hands. At this stage, it is very important to release hand pressure within a split second of feeling the hocks come through and under; if the rider's coordination is not perfect, and if the hands resist too long, the horse will hurtle against the bit and step back. It is also a good idea to remain halted for long periods of time to promote immobility. Full halts can be practised in shoulder-in, travers, renvers and half-passes to ensure even loading of the horses weight and self-carriage.

In training geldings and mares, I have had no problem obtaining perfect immobility. However, with certain stallions I have found that perfect immobility can be a problem. Some stallions will learn to halt square in perfect self-carriage and then proceed to caress their testicles by shifting their hind legs from side to side before settling in a square halt again. I have administered harsh leg and whip punishment to correct this fault, but eventually it has always recurred. Perhaps I should have had an assistant stand behind me with a bucket of ice-cold water to thrust between the stallion's hind legs upon my command! I leave this slight problem to your imagination in hopes that you will come upon a better solution.

The important factor in training full halts is to be disciplined, and to train them every day. Repetition makes perfect.

CHAPTER 18

⌐-o-⌐

The Half-Halt

⌐-o-⌐

THE HALF-HALT HAS SEVERAL PURPOSES: TO RECALL a horse to attention, to shorten his strides, to improve his self-carriage as a correction to keep him from bearing down on the bit, and as a transition from one gait to another.

Over the years I have found that half-halts can be used in three distinct ways:

1) *The direct half-halt.* The rider drives with both legs, braces the lower back and resists with both hands for a brief moment until the desired result is achieved, at which moment the driving and resisting aids must cease and resume normal use. This half-halt is strong and is used in the first stages of training. The direct half-halt can also be applied by a direct action of both hands in a sharp upward motion. This is most effective on horses that bear down against the riders hands.

2) *The diagonal half-halt.* The rider drives with both legs, braces the lower back, and acts on the outside rein only. This half-halt is employed in the later stages of training, and is especially effective in all diagonal gaits — trot, passage and piaffe. It is also the best half-halt to use when demanding greater collection in all gaits, since the outside rein is the true collecting rein.

3) *The lateral half-halt.* The rider drives with inside leg only, braces the lower back, and acts with the inside rein only.

This half-halt is most effective in the canter, since the canter is a transverse gait. The action of the rider's inside leg will help thrust the horse's inside leg forward under his mass, while the action of the rider's inside hand will effectively restrict the horse's inside hind on the downward transitions, and help keep the horse's haunches from falling in.

I will not go into the rider's coordination of aids since this has been covered in a previous chapter. However, it must be noted that when the rider's legs act, the hands may resist. When the hands act, the legs may hold the horse. When one hand acts, the other may resist to keep the bit even on the horse's tongue and bars. 'Legs without hands — hands without legs.'

The employment of the half-halt and its execution belong to the domain of equestrian tact. The timing, degree of driving, and resisting can only be acquired by the utmost feel and sensitivity. It cannot be taught, it is an inherited quality. Through long experience, most riders will acquire proper feel; some will demonstrate brilliance.

The most glaring rider faults observed are wrong timing, and lack of driving aids, which always result in loss of rhythm and tempo. The half-halt must always be asked for when the horse's hind leg is flexed, supporting his weight on the ground; this will prolong the flexion of the three joints of the leg and delay the forward extension of the joints. The action of the half-halt must affect the hind leg only, and the hand must give as soon as extension is felt. During the phase of extension and propulsion forward, the horse will resist any restraint of the rider's hands, but the prolonged flexion of the haunches brought about by the half-halt will shorten the phase of propulsion.

CHAPTER 19

—⊙—

Leg-Yielding

—⊙—

I F THERE IS A SUBJECT IN ACADEMIC EQUITATION which the riding masters of the past and present agree upon, it is that leg-yielding does not belong in classical training as a suppling exercise. Like the turn on the forehand, leg-yielding can be used in the early stages of training to teach a young horse to yield to the rider's legs. When the exercise is used to achieve this goal, it should be performed in the walk only, and with as much bend around the rider's inside (active) leg as needed, in order to allow the horse's thorax to tilt in its thoracic sling to the inside, thus facilitating the crossing of the horse's legs on four tracks to the side opposite to the direction of the bend. Leg-yielding is best performed on 20 metre circles, since the curvature of the circle will help promote bend and sideward motion. When the horse yields to both reins, the exercise should be stopped.

William Cavendish, Duke of Newcastle, may have been one of the first to realize the uselessness of leg-yielding as a suppling exercise when he wrote: 'The head in, the haunches out on a circle, brings the horse on the forehand. . . The shoulders cannot become supple if the inner hind leg does not come close and in front of the outer hind leg.' La Guérinière was greatly influenced by this statement when he invented shoulder-in!

It is obvious that in leg-yielding, when a horse is asked to move sideways on four tracks with little lateral bend, the inside hind leg cannot move forward and sideways to the centre of gravity, and the inside foreleg cannot move forward and over the outside fore. Therefore, in leg-yielding the horse will, by necessity, raise his croup, fall onto his forehand, and move sideways with loss of rhythm.

There are further disadvantages to this exercise. Since the forelegs are crossing laterally on a very narrow path, the inside fore will often hit the outside fore, which can cause splints and lameness. Also, in leg-yielding, the horse is stretched and longer in his frame than in other lateral exercise, which inhibits coordination between haunches and shoulders, and, by lack of bend and lateral displacement on narrow tracks, the hind legs cannot oscillate sideways and under, which limits any suppling effect. Furthermore, because of the narrow tracks, the rhythm of the pure gait is destroyed. To quote Gustav Steinbrecht in *Das Gymnasium Des Pferdes* (1884); 'Two track movements without correct bending and collection are always wrong exercises.'

CHAPTER 20

Shoulder-Fore

S HOULDER-FORE IS A TOUCH OF SHOULDER-IN. In shoulder-fore, the horse's inside hind hoof tracks between his forelegs.

Shoulder-fore.

This uniform, imperceptible flexion traverses the entire body of the horse and allows the rider to re-aline the narrower shoulders with the wider haunches, thus helping to straighten and correct the horse's imperfect rectitude on straight lines in all gaits, and especially in extended canters, transitions to collection and highly collected gaits, such as canter on the spot and piaffe.

Shoulder-fore is also the preparatory movement for all half-passes in the trot and canter and pirouettes in the walk, along with canter and canter departs. It should also be ridden in the collected walk; it will help prevent spoiling a great walk, as well as disguising a poor lateral, or two-beat walk. The one fault most commonly seen in shoulder-fore is too much bend in the neck. This movement must be ridden predominantly with the inside leg; in other words, a little flexion of the inside hind leg, a touch of bend in the neck.

CHAPTER 21

‿o‿

Shoulder-In

‿o‿

S HOULDER-IN IS THE SINGLE MOST IMPORTANT LATERAL exercise
in academic equitation. It brings about freedom of the horse's
shoulders, obedience to the rider's hands — resulting in lightness
of the forehand — suppleness of the horse's haunches, obedience
to the rider's legs, and engagement of the hindquarters. Longitudinal suppleness, which brings about harmonious accord between the horse's shoulders and haunches, creates improved
balance.

Explanation and Uses

‿o‿

Let me ride you through shoulder-in right to further clarify the
exercise. On the right rein, the rider braces his back and legs. He
closes his fingers on the outside rein (half-halt). At the same
time, he slips his inside (right) leg slightly behind the girth to
bend and engage the inside (right) hind leg to the outside. The
horse, his forward impulsion meeting the resisting outside rein,
will bend his shoulders to the right (inside). The rider's inside
rein and leg maintain the bend and forward motion, while the
rider's outside leg remains passive behind the girth, ready to
mobilize or restrict the hindquarters from falling to the outside.
The horse, thus bent geometrically around the rider's inside leg,
moves forward on three tracks. The horse's inside hind leg

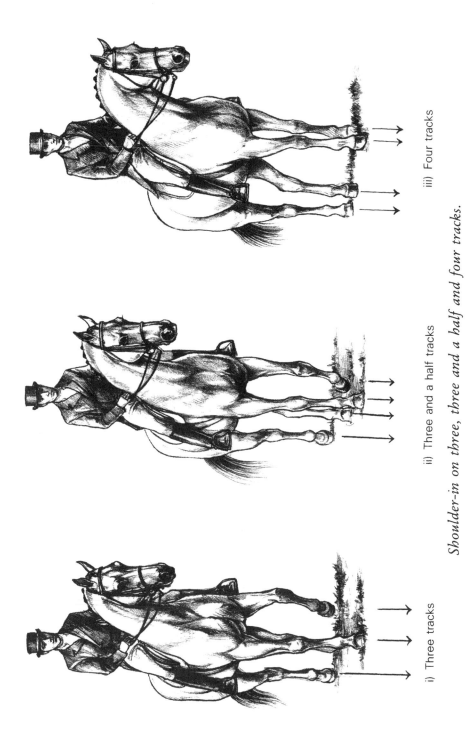

i) Three tracks

ii) Three and a half tracks

iii) Four tracks

Shoulder-in on three, three and a half and four tracks.

follows the track of the outside foreleg, while the horse's outside hind leg and right foreleg form two separate tracks of their own. In such a position, the horse finds himself obliged to lift his right fore knee to overlap it with the left foreleg. He must, at the same time, lower his right haunch in order to engage his hind leg forward and inward toward the medial plane of his body. At the same time as the inside hind leg engages, the outside shoulder extends. We thus have two distinct sets of circumstances: firstly, a suppling and strengthening effect through extensor and flexor motion of the diagonal pair, and secondly, a collecting effect, by the lowering of a haunch and elevation of a shoulder.

The important points in riding shoulder-in are to ensure that the horse's inside hind leg does not cross over the outside hind; if this occurs, the horse will have too much angle to the track and place himself in 'leg-yielding', which is wrong. The horse's inside hind must oscillate forward and under, and alight in front of the outside hind hoof, but never cross over it! The horse's neck must never be flexed beyond the point of the shoulder blade. The rider must continuously assume that the geometric bend is correct.

As the horse becomes more supple, the degree of bend can be increased to four tracks. This increased bend shortens the horse's base of support by further lowering his inside haunch and elevating his inside shoulder. The horse, now travelling on four distinct tracks with haunches and shoulders closer together, increases his degree of collection, suppleness and balance.

In addition to being a suppling and collecting exercise, shoulder-in is also used to perfect half-passes in the walk and trot; to straighten a horse in all of the gaits; to put a horse back on the rider's aids; to correct a faulty walk; to perfect the piaffe and passage, etc... The use of shoulder-in will crop up many times in future chapters of this book.

Teaching the Horse

As soon as my horses are ready for lateral work, I teach them to yield to my legs, first by teaching turns on the forehand, and later, after this exercise is perfected, by short periods of leg-yielding on a 20 metre circle in walk. As soon as the horse yields with some degree of proficiency, I stop these preparatory exercises and start teaching shoulder-in.

It is always best to teach the horse shoulder-in first to his weak or concave side (usually the left). It will be easier for the horse to oscillate and engage his inside hip joint to this side. The aids used to ride shoulder-in have already been described but in teaching this exercise it is important to remember to always maintain correct bend; not to lose rhythm or impulsion; not to overflex the horse's neck; and to make sure that the inside hind leg does not cross over the outside hind.

I always ask first for shoulder-in on a straight line along the wall of the riding hall. The wall helps maintain correct bend without allowing the horse to swing his haunches to the outside. It also allows the rider to teach the horse the use of the outside leg without having to use force. When starting this exercise on a circle, one can be dangerously lulled into a pseudo leg-yielding. Here again, as in teaching any new exercise, it is important to ask only for a few correct steps at a time, but ask often. When the horse loses rhythm and impulsion, it is not only useful to go directly on a circle to maintain bend, but also to increase impulsion; or to ride directly out of shoulder-in on a diagonal in a strong, lengthening trot. When rhythm and impulsion are lost in any lateral exercise, the horse must be ridden forward on straight lines in an energetic trot until the impulsion is restored and the lateral exercise can be attempted anew.

Counter shoulder-in can be a very effective exercise, provided it is ridden on straight lines, as a means of straightening a horse who tilts his head and has lost contact with the rider's outside rein. Counter shoulder-in is, in essence, the same exercise as shoulder-in. For example, if you ride shoulder-in on the right rein, the horse is bent around your inside (right) leg. If you then wish to ride counter shoulder-in, you simply bend the horse to the outside, towards the wall, around your new inside (left) leg. When riding counter shoulder-in, the rider must be careful not to allow the horse to increase his angle to the wall and cross his inside hind leg over his outside hind, and thus place himself in leg-yielding. The rider must therefore be aware of the increased

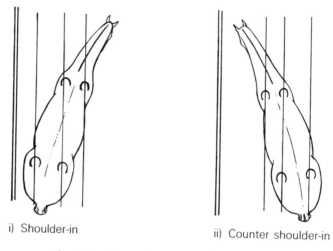

i) Shoulder-in   ii) Counter shoulder-in

Shoulder-in and counter shoulder-in.

need for his outside leg to compensate for the absence of the wall and help mobilize the horse's haunches. I do not advocate, or practice this exercise on circles, for it puts the horse onto his outside shoulder and out of proper balance. This fault can also occur on straight lines when the rider uses too much inside rein and overbends the horse in the neck.

Faults In Shoulder-In

Some common faults observed in shoulder-in are:

1) Too much bend in the horse's neck and not enough engagement of the inside hind leg. To correct this fault, the rider must use more inside leg and outside rein.

2) In shoulder-in right, one can observe at times, a tilting of the horse's head to the left (the horse's right ear is lower). This fault can be corrected in several ways: the rider can raise the inside rein momentarily, stop the exercise and ride forward for a few strides or go directly into counter shoulder-in for a few strides. The most common cause for this fault is stiffness in the right hind leg and/or in the jowl and jaw, but the fault can also be caused by a rider who does not use the outside rein correctly.

3) Loss of tempo and rhythm. This fault can be easily corrected by increased leg pressure, or by riding forward in an energetic trot until impulsion is rekindled.

4) Too much angle and not enough bend. Here the rider must maintain the bend with more outside leg and rein to prevent the horse from going into leg-yielding by crossing his inside hind leg over the outside hind leg.

Bend and Tracking

This chapter cannot be concluded without further reference to bend. When la Guérinière wrote *Ecole De Cavalerie* in 1733, he was inconsistent in the use of his words in describing the exercise he devised. According to the original text, it would seem that he prescribed riding shoulder-in on three tracks. On p. 197 he wrote:

> *La ligne des haunches doit être près de la muraille, et celle des epaules, détachée et éloignée du mur environ un pied et demi ou deux, en le tenant plié à la main ou il va.*
>
> The line of the haunches must be near to the wall and that of the shoulders detached and brought away from the wall about one hoof and a half or two, keeping him bent to the rein he is going.

This statement would indicate little lateral bend. However, the paragraph containing the above sentence is dedicated to teaching the horse shoulder-in. On p. 198 he wrote:

> *Comme in est aisé de le voir dans la figure de l'épaule en dedans, qui est au commencement de ce chapitre, et dans le plan de terre de la même leçon, qui rendront la chose encore plus sensible.*
>
> It will be easy to see by the illustration of shoulder-in at the beginning of this chapter, and by the diagram of the same lesson, which will give the subject more understanding.

The illustration referred to shows the horse and rider in shoulder-fore, not bent on three tracks; while the diagram showing the footfalls and bend, clearly shows the horse on four tracks.

I firmly believe after years of experience, that the more

supple a horse becomes, the more his shoulders can be bent to the inside to shorten the base of support, placing him on three and a half (that is, one track half a hoofprint wide) to four tracks, further increasing collection, suppleness and balance. Let the historians of the past debate, let the F.E.I. and most National Federations require that shoulder-in be ridden on three tracks in their tests. So be it... if the exercise can be correctly ridden to its ultimate bend on four tracks, it will be simplicity itself to present the movement on three tracks! What is of the utmost importance is to show the same degree of bend to both reins. It would be a bad mistake to show more bend to the horse's weak (concave) side, and less bend to the strong (convex) side.

As stated, I will perfect shoulder-in on four tracks with my horses as they progress to maximum lateral suppleness. I would like to mention, however, that I practice shoulder-in ultimately on four tracks only in the walk and trot, whereas in the canter, I restrict the exercise to three tracks. The reason for this difference is as follows. The trot being a diagonal gait, as the horse's inside hind leg engages to the medial line, the inside shoulder rises and the outside shoulder extends. The more the horse's shoulders are brought to the inside, the shorter his base of support, and the more collection increases. However, in the canter, which is a transverse gait, we have the opposite effect; as the horse's inside hind leg engages, his inside fore rises. The more the horse's shoulders are brought to the inside, the more we restrict the clear three-beat forward rhythm and flatten the movement by putting the horse on his outside shoulder. Therefore, in the canter I perform shoulder-fore, or shoulder-in on three tracks only.

I have studied the original text of *Ecole De Cavalerie* in great detail. The book gave me a wonderful inner warmth for la Guérinière. His direct approach, logic and innovations really leave one with the feeling that he was a true genius on horseback. He gives the writings of Solomon de la Broue, and the Duke of Newcastle, full credit for his invention of shoulder-in, which indicates his honesty, and, perhaps, his modesty. His explanations of other innovations are logical and direct and can be easily understood by any horseman. Perhaps the lack of detail in parts of his manuscript reflects his own lack of management of his personal life. While his two academies were held in high esteem and well patronized, he never could make ends meet and was in constant financial difficulties.

La Guérinière found many wonderful solutions, but could not solve the problem of how to make a living. This is probably the greatest accolade one could give a true artistic genius... and I am sure that when his horses reached sufficient lateral flexibility, he would put them in '*le beau pli*', on four tracks.

CHAPTER 22

⟿

Travers and Renvers

⟿

T HESE EXERCISES HAVE ALSO BEEN CALLED: *tête au mur* (head to the wall) and *croupe au mur* (croupe to the wall). In America, we often refer to the exercises as haunches in and haunches out. Since the official parlance of the F.E.I. is travers and renvers, to avoid further confusion, I will use their phraseology.

These lateral exercises are nothing more than extensions of shoulder-in, intended to give the horse increased suppleness, strength and collection. The biomechanical effects of these exercises, however, are not the same as in shoulder-in.

Travers

⟿

In travers, the horse does not engage his inside hind leg to the medial plane of his body, nor extend his outside hind, instead, he only engages his inside hind leg to the point of the hip (line of maximum lift) and places the majority of his weight on this hind leg by virtue of his weight moving across it. As a result, he increases the flexion of stifle, hock and fetlock. Because of this, maximum gymnastic benefit can only be obtained in the trot and canter; travers performed in the walk can only be a lesson in the accord of the aids.

Again, when first teaching travers, it is better to start on the horse's weak, or concave side (usually the left). To teach this exercise, it is best to start out of a corner on the left rein. The rider simply takes advantage of the horse's lateral bend in the corner, and, as he emerges to the long side of the hall, the rider pushes the horse's haunches to the inside with the outside leg, while the inside leg maintains bend and impulsion. The rider's inside rein remains passive, while the outside rein controls the degree of bend, and tempo. The movement must be on three tracks in the beginning, just as in shoulder-in. As the horse's lateral flexibility increases, so can the bend.

The important point in travers is to maintain the horse's shoulders and neck completely parallel to the wall, or track — only the horse's haunches are brought to the inside. This geometric bend gives the proper biomechanical effects of increasing weight on the horse's inside hind, which in turn produces the desired increased flexion of the three joints of the inside hind leg. Travers has little or no suppling effect on the horse's shoulders; however, the exercise is excellent to promote further lateral suppleness of the hindquarters, and collection.

Renvers

Renvers is the exact opposite exercise to travers. It has the same biomechanical effects, but instead of bringing the haunches to the inside, the haunches remain on the track and the horse's shoulders are brought to the inside. Renvers is more difficult for the horse to learn in the beginning of training, for it is not as natural for a horse to mobilize his haunches to the outside. However, once travers has been mastered, it should be performed less and less, and finally abandoned in favour of its counter lesson, renvers. We spend most of our time on horseback keeping our horses from disengaging their inside hind legs and slipping the haunches to the inside, therefore, it makes sense to favour renvers.

Renvers can be taught out of a passade, as at the Spanish Riding School. A passade is a partial piroutte ridden out of shoulder-in to produce renvers. I prefer to teach the movement

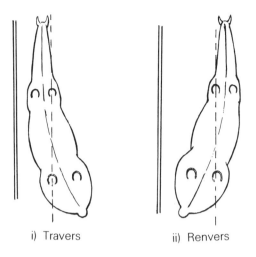

i) Travers   ii) Renvers

Travers and renvers.

as I do travers, out of a corner. When approaching the second corner of the short side, I simply displace the horse's haunches to the outside of the turn with my inside leg. Upon reaching the straight long side, I keep mobilizing the horse's haunches to the outside with my new outside leg while I maintain the bend and impulsion with my new inside leg. My inside rein is more active than in travers; it maintains inside bend, while my outside rein dictates the desired degree of bend and tempo. Here again the horse's shoulders must remain dead straight to the wall, or track. Only the haunches are brought to the outside on three tracks.

Exercises In Travers and Renvers

There are many additional exercises where travers and renvers can be ridden. I will only mention the ones that have been most helpful. Travers and renvers can be ridden on circles, and on diminishing circles where the horse is asked to track into the centre point of the circle as much as his suppleness will allow, without losing rhythm and tempo. This exercise can be performed in the trot and canter; however, in the canter it is best performed in renvers only.

Another exercise that I have found very helpful is 'forcing

the corners'. Before explaining this exercise, I would like to say a few words about voltes which may help you better understand this exercise. In the old days, voltes were smaller. The old masters were training horses of Andalusian and Arab descent, who were relatively small, being considered on average to be 2.75 metres in length. Therefore, the smallest radius possible was 2.75 metres, resulting in a circle with a diameter of 5.5 metres. Today our horses are bigger. Their average length is standardized at 3 metres therefore, the smallest radius is 3 metres, resulting in a circle of 6 metres diameter, which we refer to as a volte.

While I adhere to riding voltes correctly in tests, when forcing the corners, I ride the smallest possible circles in accordance with the horse's degree of training, suppleness and flexibility. Again, the important rule is not to lose rhythm and tempo. Forcing the corners is a very demanding exercise and should only be practiced with horses well advanced in their training – and then with utmost caution. In this exercise, the three lateral movements are used – shoulder-in, travers and renvers. To force the corner, I ride shoulder-in along the last part of the long side of the hall and, without losing bend, go into a small circle in the first corner, come out of the circle in travers, which I ride along the short side, back onto a small circle in the second corner and out of this circle in renvers. This exercise is repeated in all four corners of the riding hall, and any variation of the three lateral exercises can be used, depending upon which side of the horse needs more stretching or flexing. The important points in this exercise are to make the circles as small as possible without loss of rhythm or tempo and to keep the lateral bend even to both sides. This exercise must only be performed in the walk or trot.

I often use an easier version of the above to warm up my advanced horses. First, in the walk I will ride six strides of shoulder-in straight into six strides of renvers, back into six strides of shoulder-in, into a volte and out in shoulder-in or renvers. The number of strides, the variation of the movements and degree of lateral bend can be varied. Once these exercises have been ridden in the walk and trot on both reins, I start riding half-passes out of shoulder-in, back into shoulder-in, counter shoulder-in, or renvers. This warm up is very useful for older horses who cannot sustain a great amount of work.

CHAPTER 23

◦

Pirouettes In the Trot On Diminishing Circles

◦

O NCE THE HORSE HAS PERFECTED THE LATERAL EXERCISES of shoulder-in, travers and renvers, pirouettes in the trot are excellent exercises to further develop lateral as well as longitudinal suppleness. Pirouettes in the trot are executed in two different ways; around the shoulders and around the haunches, each having different biomechanical effects.

In the pirouette on the shoulders, for example to the right, you start on a 10 metre circle to the right in shoulder-in and, while maintaining the bend, gradually reduce the size of the circle until the horse's inside front hoof moves up and down on the spot, while the other three legs pivot around it to the outside. This exercise transfers more weight to the horse's forehand and stretches his muscles by a hollowing action of the back.

In the pirouette on the haunches, you start on a 10 metre circle in renvers and gradually diminish the size of the circle until the inside hind foot trots on the spot, while the other legs pivot around it to the outside. This exercise transfers more weight to the horse's haunches and flexes his muscles by a rounding action of the back.

These two pirouettes, when ridden alternately, on both bends, help put the horse on the bit; they develop suppleness by stretching and flexing the musculature and develop balance by alternating weight placement. Pirouettes in the trot are also valuable exercises for horses who are unusually convex to one

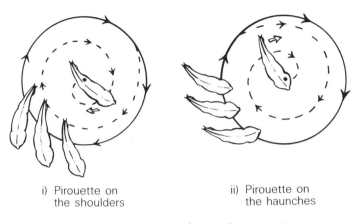

i) Pirouette on
the shoulders

ii) Pirouette on
the haunches

Pirouettes in trot on diminishing circles.

side. For instance, if a horse is convex right, pirouettes on the shoulders in shoulder-in right and pirouettes in renvers right will help straighten the horse and improve his rectitude.

Another lateral exercise to help horses who are strongly convex to one side, is to ride 'shoulders and haunches in' on straight lines to the convex side. For instance, if a horse is convex right, you bend the shoulders and haunches evenly around your inside (right) leg, and move forward on a straight line until the horse relaxes and gives to your left leg and right rein. This exercise can also be ridden on a circle with the bend to the inside. I do not recommend riding shoulder and haunches in on a circle with the bend to the outside, since this puts too much weight on the horse's outside shoulder and will disrupt his balance.

CHAPTER 24

— ◦ —

The Half-Pass In the Walk and Trot

— ◦ —

T HE HALF-PASS IS THE CULMINATION OF ALL LATERAL work. It must be started only after perfection has been attained in shoulder-in, travers and renvers. All half-passes must be started

Half-pass in trot.

out of shoulder-fore and, since the horse's haunches are much wider than the shoulders, the rider must be careful to obtain the correct alignment. It is very important that the shoulders be brought a little more into the direction of the movement. In the half-pass, the horse travels forward and sideways bent around the rider's inside leg. Diagonal aids are used; inside leg at the girth to maintain forward movement and shoulder-fore bend, outside leg behind the girth to displace the horse forward and sideways. I emphasise forward first, for it is impossible for the horse to move sideways in the correct bend unless his first movement is forward. The outside shoulder and leg cannot cross over the inside foreleg in correct bend, balance, rhythm and tempo, unless its first movement is forward. The outside rein maintains the degree of collection needed, while the inside rein maintains the necessary bend. The hands must act softly and be always ready to give.

Early Work

In the first stages of training half-passes, it is important to use as long a diagonal as possible to be able to ride forward and make any corrections needed. It is a mistake to train the tighter half-passes, where greater collection is needed, at the start. All horses, no matter how good their rectitude, have the tendency to execute half-passes with more ease to one side than the other. In general, they will find it easier going to their concave or weak sides, and they will also tend to lead with their haunches in that direction. They will have more difficulty going to their convex, or strong sides, and will drag their haunches in that direction.

It is easier to start training the half-pass from the centre line back to the long sides, then from the long sides back to the centre line, and then across the entire diagonal. A horse who tends to lead with his quarters should be ridden for a few strides straight in shoulder-in to the opposite side when reaching the long side, or centre line. Also, the rider must exert stronger contact with the inside leg and inside rein and make sure that the outside rein is worked straight back and not used as a leaning rein against the horse's neck. On the other hand, if a horse tends to drag his quarters, he must be ridden for a few steps forward in renvers, and the rider must increase the pressure of the outside leg, moving it a fraction farther back on the flank. When the half-passes are executed correctly, they should always be finished in shoulder-fore to the opposite side. This is the best way to re-establish engagement of the inside hind leg and is good preparation for the counter changes of hand and zigzags. When the horse loses his bend during a half-pass, he must be ridden forward in shoulder-fore to the same side for a few strides to re-establish the bend, and then sideways again. This correction should be repeated as many times as necessary during the same half-pass.

More Advanced Work

Once the horse can execute these wider half-passes without loss of bend, balance, rhythm, or tempo, then it is time to ask for half-passes as in the higher level tests; the short half-pass, the counter changes of hand and the zigzags. The only difference is the greater degree of collection and suppleness required.

The counter changes of hand, as presently called for in dressage tests, are ridden from the long side to X and back to the long side, and from the long side across the half arena and back to the long side. When riding the first counter change, it is important to reach the centre line one stride in front of X to re-establish the new bend on the second stride and to start back to the track during the third stride. The straightness and accuracy of these three strides on the centre line is important. In the counter changes across the half arena, the horse must arrive one stride in front of the marker in order to establish the new bend during the second stride and move smoothly back to the long side during the third stride. Zigzags in the trot are usually called to be performed from the centre line to the quarter lines. As the tests increase in difficulty, these counter changes will be increased in number to four. In the zigzags, the rider must not be in any hurry to re-establish the new bend, for most horses will start anticipating the change in direction. It is a good idea when

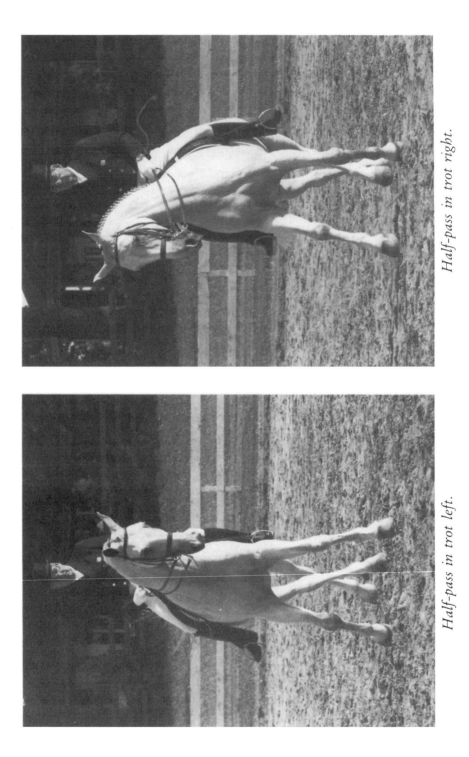

Half-pass in trot left.

Half-pass in trot right.

training zigzags to ride past the quarter line before re-establishing the new bend in shoulder-fore.

A fault that often appears at this stage is tilting of the horse's head. This fault is usually the result of stiffness in the haunches, or in the case of some older horses, the beginning of arthritis in the joints of the legs. Some trainers attempt to straighten this fault with rein aids, but I have had more success by riding forward in an extended trot for several strides until the horse straightens his head-carriage. I have found that when a horse tilts his head to one side, it is almost always the hind leg to the opposite side which needs suppling. Here again, we must revert to the basics and work on circles, shoulder-in and renvers.

The most common rider fault when performing half-passes is not letting the weight shift in the direction of the movement. To counteract this fault, it is helpful to keep the inside leg in better contact, and to look out of the corner of the eyes in the direction of the movement, since the human body will follow the line of sight. Some riders collapse the inside hip and allow the inside hand to cross the withers, which is as bad a mistake as letting the outside rein cross over the horse's neck as a leaning rein. Overbending the horse's neck is another mistake often seen; the horse's neck must never be bent beyond the point of the shoulder.

Other errors in half-pass include loss of impulsion and uneven strides. When the former occurs the horse should then be woken up with a few strides of extended trot, and then ridden in half-passes in the working trot on long diagonals until the necessary impulsion is re-established. Uneven strides are often a serious problem, for the first stage of lameness will always reveal itself in half-pass work in the trot before it is apparent in any other gait or exercise. Consulting a veterinarian would be the best cure for this problem.

CHAPTER 25

⸺◦⸻

Half-Passes and Zigzags In the Canter

⸺◦⸻

I N A CANTER HALF-PASS, THE HORSE DOES NOT CROSS HIS LEGS
as in the walk and trot; he simply 'hops' from one lateral to
the other. This exercise, therefore, has little or no gymnastic
benefit and is simply a demonstration of dexterity. The canter
half-passes must start in shoulder-fore to create the proper bend.
A horse will tend to drag his haunches going to his dominant, or
convex side, and will tend to lead with his haunches going to his
weak, or concave side. In canter half-passes horses tend to transfer
too much weight to their forehands, so it is important for the
rider to maintain a collected frame with the engagement of the
haunches. The aids for riding canter half-passes are the same as
in the walk and trot. However, the rider will need a little more
inside rein to encourage the forward/sideways hops.

There are four basic half-pass movements called for at
different levels of competition, and we shall examine them in
ascending order.

The Half-Pass

⸺◦⸻

Half-passes can be ridden from the long side to the centre line,
and from the centre line back to the long side. When riding a
half-pass from the centre line back to the track, either a simple

Half-pass in canter.

change or a flying change will be called for in order to re-establish the true canter. In either case, the rider must plan to come back to the track approximately one horse's length in front of the marker where the change is asked for, in order to execute the change when the rider's knee and shoulder are parallel to the marker. When riding a half-pass from the track to the centre line, changes of lead are rarely required. The important thing here is to finish the half-pass exactly on the centre line and to ride straight ahead. In these single half-passes, accuracy is of the essence.

Half-pass in canter right.

Half-pass in canter left.

The Full Pass

A full pass is, as the name suggests, a pass across the entire width of the hall. To ride a full pass to the right rein, say across the diagonal M−X−K, the rider starts planning at A and places the horse in shoulder-fore while riding through the corner, and as the rider's knee and shoulder come even with M, the horse is moved sideways and performs a full pass across the diagonal. The horse must be brought back to the track, one length in front of K, and asked for a flying change from right to left at K. When practising these full-passes, it is a good idea to forget the flying change, and ride through the corner in counter-canter, or to ask for the change at A or C. This will prevent the horse from anticipating.

The Counter Change of Hand

The counter change of hand in the canter is basically the same as in the trot except that, in the canter, there are two flying changes involved which must be executed straight and at the markers, and this demands proper preparation and accuracy. In riding a counter change from the right rein, for example between the letters M−X−F, the horse must be prepared in shoulder-fore one stride before M, and leave M in a half-pass to the centre line, one length in front of X, to allow one straight stride, a flying change from right to left at X, another stride straight in shoulder-fore left, and a half-pass back to the track one length in front of F, so that the next flying change from right to left can be made as the rider's knee and shoulder come even with the marker. The counter change of hand is not a difficult exercise, providing that the rider thinks ahead and concentrates on the execution of the movement.

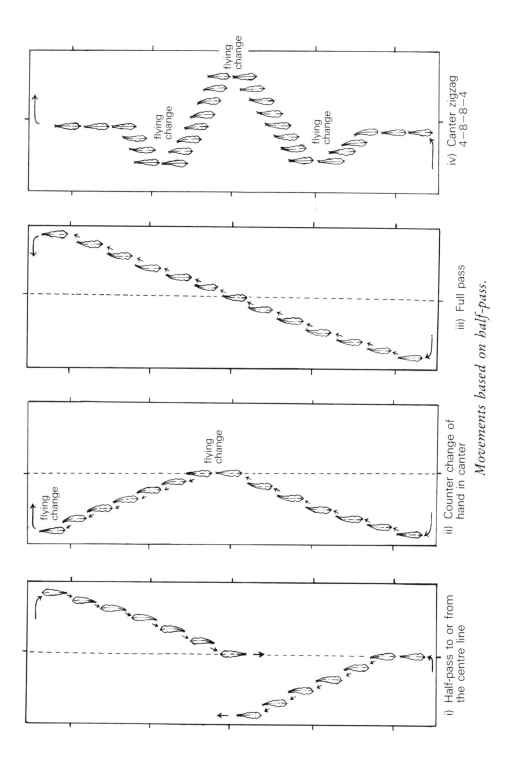

Movements based on half-pass.

i) Half-pass to or from the centre line

ii) Counter change of hand in canter

iii) Full pass

iv) Canter zigzag 4–8–8–4

The Canter Zigzag

The canter zigzag places increased demands on dexterity and requires more training than all other half-passes, but is not difficult for horses with good canters. Over the years, the F.E.I. has proposed two zigzags; one of 4−8−8−4 strides in the intermediate tests and one of 3−6−6−6−6−3 strides in the Grand Prix test. These short half-passes must be executed from side to side of the centre line, and cover the entire arena between the letters D and G. They must be executed in balance to the same distance either side of the centre line; the horse must maintain correct bend and rhythm and keep his haunches parallel to the centre line.

The crux of the problem in the zigzag lies in the straightening of the horse's body in the last two strides of the half-pass and the flying change back into the new direction. It is not necessary to study the last two strides of the half-pass and the flying change back in the new half-pass in slow motion: suffice it to say that, in the zigzag, it is necessary to think of riding the last two strides straight ahead. After a short period of training, the horse will gradually straighten his body when asked to go straight during the last two strides, and make a graceful, balanced flying change back into the new direction, which becomes the first stride of the new half-pass.

Let us ride through a zigzag of 4−8−8−4 strides from the right rein. As we come to the end of the long side, we start preparing our turn at A on the centre line. Approximately one horse's length in front of A, we start a smooth turn onto the centre line and ride a few strides very straight to D, where we start our half-pass of four strides to the right. We count one, two sideways; three, four straight (our horse gradually straightens his body without any further help from us), and then we ask for a flying change from right to left in the new direction, and count one and sideways two, three, four, five, six, and seven, eight, forward and flying change from left to right back in the new direction; one, and sideways two, three, four, five, six, and straight seven, eight and flying change from right to left; one, and two, three, four sideways to G. We ride a few straight strides to C and turn smoothly left. If in a test where a flying change is asked for at G, we must then ride the fourth half-pass one length in front of G to execute the change at G, and have sufficient room to ride a few straight strides to C.

The zigzag 3−6−6−6−6−3 is executed exactly the same way. In this zigzag, however, the horse will be slightly more collected and the changes in direction happen faster. As a matter of fact, this zigzag can be easier for a horse with a very good canter, for the shorter half-passes will automatically tend to collect him in better self-carriage, and he will show better balance in the changes, and smoother dexterity. In this zigzag, it is wise to ride the second half-pass of six strides just short of X to ensure sufficient room to finish the second half of the movement to G.

There are several problems that can crop up during zigzags. One of the most common is anticipation; many horses start to anticipate the flying change, and change in direction. The best way to correct this fault is simply to ride more strides to the side. If you are practising a zigzag of 4−8−8−4, train it 8−12−12−8, or whatever feels best. As stated, the horse must maintain correct bend and rhythm, keep his haunches parallel to the centre line, and move to exactly the same distance to either side of the centre line. Since all horses will have a tendency to go farther over to one side of the line than the other, this possible fault can only be controlled by the rider, who would be well advised never to take the eyes off C, and maximize concentration on good ring management.

Other faults often observed in competition can be related to the horse's conformation. For instance, a small horse with a short canter stride will have difficulty covering sufficient ground forward to end up correctly at G. In this case, starting the half-pass one or two strides past D and riding more forward in a slightly higher tempo will help. There are three judges on the far short side and only two on the long sides who might see what we are up to. In actual fact, a judge cannot assess the number of strides of the first half-pass until the first step is visibly sideways. Most judges are more concerned with the number of steps than where they actually start. With a big horse with a long canter stride, we have the opposite problem. Where we must really concentrate on riding is our turn up the centre line in shoulder-fore, and after one stride, start the zigzag, regardless of our location to D. The horse will have to be collected in the canter and ridden sideways as much as he can go without loss of balance and rhythm. With such horses, it is absolutely necessary to execute the first half of the zigzag well short of the centre of the arena at X, for the second half of the zigzag will be much harder for such horses, and you do not want to have to box your way into the President of the Jury's lap at C!

I have always found it easier training zigzags cross-country either on a long wide bridle path, or a mown field where I can use the tracings of the mower for my centre line. The freedom to move forward without any restriction makes it easier for all horses to find their bearing, balance, and rhythm. When you can canter on straight for a mile or more, it is easy to maintain impulsion and the horse's interest — it becomes a little game; now you do, now you don't . . .

CHAPTER 26

—◦—

The Rein-Back

—◦—

THE REIN-BACK IS ONE OF THE LAST SUPPLING exercises I incorporate into my gymnastic routines. A horse should not be asked to rein back until he has become very supple. All too often this exercise is practised too early in training, and as a result, has adverse effects on the horse's body and mind. The main benefits derived from a properly executed rein-back are the further suppling of the hindquarters and back muscles, the promotion of balance and tactful coordination of the rider's legs and hands.

Teaching the Horse

—◦—

The walk is a transverse lateral gait, but when the horse is asked to walk to the rear, the gait changes to a diagonal rhythm. As a result, the rein-back can be asked for by direct or diagonal aids. The rider applies gradual leg pressure to create forward impulsion, while almost simultaneously applying resistance through the hands. Either by direct or diagonal contact, the horse meets this resistance and immediately transfers body weight to the rear. When the point of his haunches passes to the rear over the line of maximum lift, this activates the hind legs and the horse walks to the rear in diagonal rhythm. As soon as the horse responds to the rear, the rider must relax leg pressure and simply keep a very light diagonal or direct contact with the horse's mouth. The steps must remain straight, even, and calm, and have the same elevation as in the forward walk. As soon as the desired number of backward steps are obtained, the rider applies light leg pressure, ceases all hand action, and the horse shifts his weight forward, and without hesitation, walks forward. The rider must maintain a straight, supple, and light seat. The upper body must never lean forward or backwards to influence the movement of the horse.

The rein-back can be taught out of the collected walk or the halt; it should, however, always be started to the horse's convex side (usually the right). Place the horse on the right rein along the wall of the riding hall so that the horse's concave side is against the wall. This will keep the horse straight in the beginning of training and prevent him from spreading his hind legs.

Overcoming Faults

Several faults appear in the rein-back, especially when it is asked for too early in training. The horse will come over the bit, block his back, and walk to the rear in short, uneven steps, or will drop behind the bit and walk back in fast, uneven steps. Both faults are best corrected outside on a hill. If the horse has a tendency to come over the bit, make him back up the hill. The incline will help the horse extend his legs to the rear while lowering his neck. If the horse tends to come behind the bit, reverse the procedure and make him back down the hill; this will shorten his stride and raise his neck. The other common fault that crops up is a total lack of regard for the rider's aids. Here the horse runs backward behind the bit, out of control. In this case, the rider must apply strong leg aids to get the horse back in front of the legs; and most likely not ask for any more rein-backs until the horse is further advanced in training. All horses have a tendency to rush backwards to some degree, for their bodies start the rearward move before their legs activate to establish balance. Furthermore, as the diagonal pair of legs are on the ground to support the horse's weight, his body is still moving backwards; therefore, the horse's legs are constantly attempting to catch up with the body.

The 'Swing'

Once the horse can rein-back in even, straight steps without any resistance, he should be taught the exercise of the swing. At this stage the horse will offer you the swing as a present. The swing is a prescribed number of backward steps, immediately and un-hesitatingly followed by a prescribed number of forward steps, again followed by a prescribed number of backward steps and forward again in a transition to the walk, trot or canter. The important thing in teaching this movement is to ensure that the steps are of the number asked, straight, and in rhythm. To obtain the exact number of steps back and forth will simply demand practise. It is important to vary the number to avoid anticipation, and to make sure that they flow without any hesitation.

The key to performing a correct rein-back, or swing, in competition starts with the halt. The horse must come into the halt very square with hocks well engaged. This will allow the proper transfer of weight and balance to the rear, thus allowing the first step backwards to be correct, and all others to follow in perfect sequence.

CHAPTER 27

Flying Changes

FLYING CHANGES ARE NOTHING MORE THAN CANTER departs in the air. To be correct and artistic, the change must be very straight and springing forward with impulsion and expression. The hind legs must come through almost to the line of maximum thrust. The shoulders must be supple, allowing the forelegs forward extended expression. When flying changes are properly trained in the final stage, the rider should be able to ride them in the medium canter. The horse must perform flying changes jumping 'in front' of rather than 'under' his rider!

The Movement and the Aids

In order to understand more about the flying change, it is necessary to understand the sequence of the canter stride before, during and after the change. Once the horse's inner foreleg has pushed off after the third beat of the canter, the phase of suspension follows, during which he must change his lead to prevent the outside hind leg from taking its load first. Since it did up to now, greater load must be put on the leg that was formerly the inside leg, making it touch down earlier. The other leg, now carrying the same weight, swings forward for a longer time and alights later, so that the two hind legs have interchanged their roles. The

A) Aid given at this point

B)

C)

D)

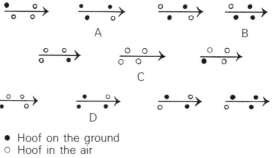

● Hoof on the ground
○ Hoof in the air

Flying changes.

flying change is initiated by the hind legs and finishes with the forelegs. Therefore, as stated earlier, the flying change can be considered as a new canter depart, and the aids for the flying changes are the same as for the canter depart; outside leg behind the girth to suggest, inside leg at the girth to demand. The aids must be applied as soon as the principal diagonal is grounded and not wait until the time of suspension – which would be too late. The aids must remain quiet and subtle. The rider's legs close to the horse's flanks (inside leg at the girth, outside leg slightly behind), allowing quick, supple, invisible action. I put more emphasis on my inside leg, for I have found that I can make my changes straighter with more forward thrust from the horse's new inside hind. Swinging the outside leg back and forth on the horse's flanks can only disrupt the horse's balance and straightness. The rider's hands must remain quiet and simply restrain the forward thrust enough to keep the desired tempo, engagement and straightness of the head and neck carriage. The rider's seat must remain vertical and supple in the saddle. If deep and supple, it will automatically follow the horse's movement without disrupting the balance of the forward jumps. The upper body must never swing from side to side. The rider's aids must remain invisible. 'An artist achieves his greatest effects by using the maximum economy of gesture.' (Waldemar Seunig)

Teaching the Horse

I start the basic development work for flying changes during the second phase and do not ask for changes until I reach the third phase of my training programme. I have found through experience, that it is best to wait until the horse has reached a high degree of suppleness, strength and self-carriage. In certain cases, when a horse has a very good canter and shows talent for flying changes, I start teaching them much earlier, before he has reached a high degree of suppleness. At this stage, a horse will perform straighter changes initially than later when he becomes very supple.

Flying changes must never be trained by rupture of balance, throwing the horse from side to side. The basic training must

Flying changes − the moment of transition.

(i) The moment of change from left to right.

(ii) Change to canter right.

start on circles, along the wall and across the diagonal in transitions trot, canter, trot; walk, canter, walk, and then build up to simple changes at X, and along the wall of the riding hall. At this stage, very careful attention must be paid to the canter depart. To canter on, I *suggest* with my outside leg and *demand* the transition with my inside leg at the girth. Within a short period, the horse will strike off to my inside leg only. I use my hands as little as possible; a touch of the outside rein maintains collection. The canter departs can be made out of shoulder-fore initially to ensure that the inside hind leg does not swing or deviate to the inside. If the eventual flying changes are to be dead straight, then the canter departs must be straight and flawless from the beginning.

As I reach the third phase of my training programme, I start to ask for successive simple changes — walk eight steps, canter eight strides, alternating leads left, right; right, left. When the eights are established, calm, forward and straight, I move on to sequences of five, four, three and eventually two strides. If the horse shows any sign of nervousness, the exercise must be stopped and calm re-established before recommencing. During this stage of training, I also ask for canter departs out of the full halt, and rein-backs; again alternating leads.

Once these simple changes have been perfected, I ask for one flying change. If I am working with a highly spirited horse, I usually choose to ask for the first change at the end of a half circle of 10 metres, or on the short diagonal where I can use the wall to restrain the forward jump instead of having to use a strong half-halt, which would restrict the new inside hind leg from swinging through to its fullest engagement. On the other hand, if I have a lazy horse, I will counter canter the long side of the arena and ask for the flying change at the entrance of the corner. This gives me more straightness and the needed impulsion. I never ask for changes on a circle, since one cannot execute a straight change on a curved line. Flying changes performed on a circle serve as a guise for bad flying changes. Most horses will change leads with more ease from right to left, so it is best to start asking for the first change from the right rein. If the horse shows great difficulty in changing from left to right, we must pause to examine the cause. Most of the time it is a fault of rectitude. If the horse in question is dominant on his right lateral, he will canter with greater ease on his left lead. This is primarily because he tries to evade bending to the right, and his right hind hoof will alight slightly in front of the left and this will traverse his haunches ever so slightly to the left. Thus, the right hind leg lacks suppleness. When this fault occurs and persists, the best correction is back to the basic lateral suppling exercises in the trot and perfecting the counter-canter.

Faults and Corrections

Other difficulties that occur, and their corrections are:

1) Changing late from behind. This problem, as explained earlier, is usually a fault of rectitude. If a horse changes late behind, say from right to left, I have found that by riding to the left rein along the wall of the hall and asking for changes in a very collected canter, with as much flexion in the hind legs as possible, and good impulsion, I can correct the late change after a short period. The wall helps maintain straightness and the collection needed for the forward jump of the right hind leg. Another exercise that is very effective in dealing with this problem, is to put the horse on a 20 metre circle in walk and ask for canter departs out of half pirouettes. It is important to ask for the strike-off during the last walk stride of the pirouette, with the inside leg only. This helps promote the forward thrust of the horse's inside hind leg. It goes without saying that the basic problem of rectitude must be continually worked on by gymnastic exercises in the trot. If the problem persists, a veterinarian should be consulted. Weak stifles or fusing hocks can often lie at the root of the problem, and medical relief will be a real help.

2) Crooked or swinging changes. Most of the time when I encounter this problem, it is on horses already trained in flying changes by other people. Again, the horse's rectitude must be considered, together with weaknesses in basic training. I have had good results correcting this problem by using the wall of the hall to help restrain the side-to-side

swing, and riding the changes as forward as possible. The increased tempo and impulsion force the hind legs more forward under the horse and keep him straighter. I also emphasise the stronger use of my inside leg at the girth, and a lot of counter-canter along the wall.

3) High in the croup. Flying changes performed with a high croup and thus on the forehand can be the result of the horse's conformation (high croup) or lack of suppleness in the hind legs. To correct this fault, I ride the changes on the diagonal in an energetic, collected canter, placing as many half-halts as necessary to keep the horse from transferring his centre of gravity too far forward. I have also found it helpful to ride to the end of the diagonal, ask for a half pirouette and ride back and then make a few changes, finishing the diagonal in another half pirouette back again. The pirouettes help re-establish collection and flexion of the hind legs.

4) Over the bit. This fault is easily corrected by reverting to the simple changes, especially through the walk, which tends to put a horse back on the bit. Then I ask for one flying change at X on both leads until the single changes are perfect and on the bit.

5) Rushing and anticipating. Sometimes backing off momentarily in training the changes is helpful. In general, I have had success overcoming this problem by counter-cantering the short side of the hall to put the horse back on my aids and interrupting the lesson with many periods of walk and relaxation. Ask for little in the beginning, but ask often. When a horse anticipates the flying change, it is wise to check the straightness of the neck and head. The rider must also make sure that outside leg contact remains on the horse's flank a little longer until the new change is asked for. Also, never ask for a change in the same place twice.

I often wonder whether the exercise of flying changes at every stride is art or circus! Certainly we do not see horses at play in the field changing leads every stride. Surely, the skipping rhythm of the gait does nothing to improve the horse's canter. Considering the emphasis the F.E.I. places on flying changes at every stride in their tests, we must assume that they become the

Flying changes every stride.

(i) *The moment of suspension, when the change to the right comes through.*

(ii) *Change to the right.*

(iii) The moment of suspension, when the new change to the left comes through.

(iv) Change to the left.

proof of the rider's dexterity and the horse's responsiveness.

Teaching the changes every stride is relatively easy. First, I assume that my changes every second stride are perfected; straight forward, clean and on the bit. At this stage, I will take the counter-canter (usually right) and ask one change every stride: right − left. Immediately upon success, I reward and walk, and start again. After a few days, when the horse is confirmed in the single change along the wall; right, left and left, right, I then progress to the frontier of the problem − every stride: right − left − right. When the horse can perform these three changes at every stride on both reins, it will be fairly easy to obtain five. At this point, I start asking for the changes on the diagonals, and usually from here on it will be very easy to obtain as many successive changes as I want. In the beginning of training, if the horse has trouble changing from behind, it is very helpful to take the horse on the diagonal or centre line of the hall, and ask for a half, or full pirouette, and immediately coming out of the pirouette, ask for three or more changes. What takes the utmost patience is not to ask the horse to cover more ground per stride than he can give. Some horses take many months of training before they establish the balance and timing they need to show their fullest potential, which must be long, ground-covering, flying leaps, performed in a very forward canter.

Finally, I would like to say that it is best not to ask for too much too fast in training flying changes. It is best to work changes only on days when we schedule their training, and to be content with the slightest progress. Start with a fresh horse and end the session on a happy note. Never tire the horse by asking more than he can give, and remember the age-old axiom 'The rider's hands are only as good as his seat.' The less you have to use your hands, and the more your hips and seat can follow and influence the forward movement without allowing the torso to move, the better the flying changes of lead will be. In competition ride the changes forward in a tempo above that of the collected canter for more expression.

CHAPTER 28

◦

Pirouette In the Walk

◦

T HE WALK PIROUETTE IS THE MOTHER OF THE CANTER pirouette. It is first trained as a turn on the haunches, which in turn is the forerunner of the working canter pirouette. Since the walk pirouette can only be performed in the collected walk, it is not a good idea to ask for walk pirouettes in the early stages of training. The turn on the haunches, however, can be performed in the working walk and can, therefore, be taught in the first stages of training. This exercise will help increase the horse's response to the rider's aids, as well as lay the foundation for all pirouettes.

The turn on the haunches must be prepared in shoulder-fore to create the necessary bend around the rider's inside leg. The horse's haunches are controlled by the rider's outside leg, which has the responsibility of displacing the horse forward/sideways in a small circle around the inside hind leg in perfect four-beat rhythm. The rider's inside leg maintains the rhythm and tempo. The outside rein maintains the degree of collection and tempo required, while the inside rein helps the horse forward/sideways. The number of steps required to complete the 180 degree turn will depend on the horse's natural walk stride. The important thing is to take as many, or as few steps as needed not to interrupt the four-beat rhythm of the walk.

I start training the turn of the haunches on a large square, using the four corners of the square as a one-quarter turn. Once the horse responds to this exercise, I ask for one-half turns across the short side of the hall, and whenever possible, in front of mirrors to check visually the activity of the hindquarters. As the horse progresses in training and is ready to be collected in the walk, I ask for half pirouettes along the wall of the hall and on a straight line across the short side in front of a mirror, to ensure absolute straightness and the activity of the inside hind leg on the spot. The faults most often seen in this exercise are:

1) Loss of rhythm and tempo. In the walk pirouette, as in all pirouettes, the rhythm and tempo must never change. When this occurs, it is best corrected by going back to the turn on the haunches, where you can ask for more forward movement to maintain rhythm and tempo.

2) Haunches swinging to the outside. This fault is usually caused by rider error. The half pirouette must be started when the horse's outside fore is at rest on the ground, and the rider will need more outside leg to mobilize the haunches and more inside leg pressure to counteract the increased demands of the outside leg in order to maintain rhythm and tempo.

3) Inside hind leg sticking. In essence, this fault is closely related to loss of rhythm and tempo, and can best be corrected by increased pressure of the rider's inside leg. If this does not suffice, the rider must ride more forward/sideways.

4) Hind legs crossing. This fault can be caused by lack of bend or balance, or the horse's haunches falling too much to the inside. This fault can be best corrected by increasing the bend of shoulder-fore going into the pirouette, and if this does not help, return to training the turn on the haunches.

5) Not completing the 180 degree turn. The horse must not be allowed to go forward as early as in the canter pirouette. The natural impulsion in the collected walk necessitates that the last stride remain on the spot and the horse not be allowed to go forward on the straight line until his body is aligned exactly with the new direction.

CHAPTER 29

⌐◦⌐

Pirouettes In the Canter

⌐◦⌐

I T IS SAID THAT 'YOU CAN JUDGE A RIDER'S ABILITY by the way he or she rides a pirouette', and I concur with this. Of all the classical exercises, the full pirouette surely demands the most equestrian tact. In a properly executed pirouette, the horse, in shoulder-fore position, canters 360 degrees around his inside hind leg in six to eight strides maintaining exact three-beat rhythm. The inside hind foot must make its beats on the same spot. The hind legs are flexed and support the majority of the weight. The forehand, rising off the ground, must show suppleness and great expression. One should have the impression that the horse can canter straight out of a pirouette at any time in perfect balance, rhythm and without loss of impulsion.

Sequence of Footfall

⌐◦⌐

The canter sequence for the pirouette is as follows: the outside forefoot strikes off and transfers weight to the inside fore, which lifts the forehand up and sideways. After this phase of suspension, the outside hind leg engages to take over the load and continues the sideward turn. The inside hind then engages forward to play its role and almost immediately transfers its weight to the outside fore. It is the outside hind that carries the greatest load in the

Canter pirouette to the right (front view).

Canter pirouette to the right (rear view).

pirouette, and thus plays the greatest role. The number of canter leaps in a pirouette varies from horse to horse, usually being between six and eight. Although as many strides as necessary must be performed to maintain the proper balance and rhythm, usually eight will be sufficient.

The Rider's Aids

The rider's aids in the pirouette are diagonal; inside leg at the girth to maintain impulsion and bend, outside leg to mobilize the haunches and help displace the shoulders around the axis. The inside rein acts to maintain the bend and help the sideward leaps, while the outside rein helps to maintain collection. The inside hand can be carried a little higher to help maintain the engagement of the hindquarters and help the sideways motion. The outside rein must always work straight back to the rider's outside hip; it must never cross over the horse's neck. This is important to keep the horse's haunches from swinging out.

Teaching the Horse

The pirouette must never be taught on the spot. Only working pirouettes can be ridden in the beginning. A working pirouette allows the horse to mark his canter leaps with his inside hoof within a 2 metre circle instead of on the spot. As the horse progresses and acquires more suppleness and strength, the 2 metre circle is made smaller and smaller until the inside hind hoof can mark its canter leaps on the same spot without loss of bend, balance, rhythm and impulsion. It is wise when practising pirouettes (even when the horse attains perfection), not to ask for them on the spot all the time, but to ride working pirouettes, which put much less strain on the three joints of the hind legs. The horse must remain fresh and happy to show expression. It is very important not to overtrain pirouettes!

There are many different ways of introducing pirouettes; the important thing is to find the method best suited for the horse. I have found that horses who have reached a sufficient degree of suppleness and strength in their hind legs can be best trained on a diminishing circle. Again, we must consider the horse's rectitude and start the working pirouettes to his easier side. If the horse is dominant right, he will usually find working pirouettes to the left easier, primarily because he can tilt his thorax left with greater ease, and his outside (right) hind has more thrust. In riding the diminishing circle, it is important to mobilize the horse's haunches and to put the horse in renvers canter, if necessary, to prevent him from deviating his haunches to the outside of the circle. I start my diminishing circle in the middle of the riding hall on a 10 metre circle and decrease the radius as much as I can without losing bend, balance, rhythm and impulsion. If I feel that I am reaching the threshold of the horse's limitations, I ride straight out of the working pirouette before the horse has a chance to falter, and I start again. When the horse has gained a fair amount of proficiency to his easy side, I start my diminishing circles to the difficult side.

Pirouettes can be taught effectively in renvers canter, especially to horses that are not yet strong enough for the diminishing circle. However, I like to get away from the renvers position as soon as possible, or not use it at all, for in competition, a pirouette prepared in renvers usually results in a deduction in score. I always use shoulder-fore to prepare pirouettes whenever possible. It is the classical way, and will be better rewarded by knowledgeable judges. However, to train pirouettes in renvers, I placed the horse in renvers 3 metres from the wall along the long side of the hall and, upon reaching the first corner, I ask for a three-quarter pirouette to the outside, coming out of the pirouette in renvers canter, and then I ask for a second three-quarter pirouette at the next corner. I then canter the long side in renvers and pass the third corner in this bend without asking for a pirouette. I then straighten the horse and ask for a flying change back to the true canter. Obviously, the wall helps restrain the horse's forward motion, the renvers bend helps mobilize the haunches and, by riding a third corner without asking for a three-quarter pirouette, I eliminate the chance of anticipation.

Almost the same exercise can be ridden in counter-canter 4 to 6 metres from the wall. Upon reaching the corner on the short side, place the horse in shoulder-fore and ask for a half pirouette to the outside, back to the wall on the long side of the hall. This exercise is very effective, and very good for horses that do not have the tendency to deviate their haunches to the outside, since we can prepare the pirouette in shoulder-fore.

The exercise I prefer and practise the most is the pirouette on a 20 metre circle. Again, I start to the horse's easier side. I establish good rhythm and balance in shoulder-fore canter then, when ready, I ask for a working half pirouette to the inside on the centre line, counter-canter the circle back to the track, and ask for a flying change and repeat. As soon as I can obtain a half pirouette on the spot, I start riding full working pirouettes on the centre line of the circle. When I want to change rein on the circle, I simply ask for a half pirouette back to the new direction. The curvature of the circle helps maintain shoulder-fore bend and the engagement of the inside hind leg. I have found this exercise very helpful and return to it often with all my horses.

During the preparatory training of pirouettes, I like to ask for a few strides of canter on the spot (half a hoof width forward at each stride). I usually start this exercise after riding cross-country on my return to the stable when the horse's impulsion is lively. I only ask for a few strides in the beginning, eventually building up to no more than eight. It is important not to ask for more collection than the horse can give. Straightness, rhythm and impulsion must never be lost. Again, if I feel that I am reaching the threshold of the horse's limitation, I ride forward before the horse falters. Later in the riding hall, I ask for a few steps along the wall, on the diagonals and centre line. I have found that the more you collect, the more you have to ride shoulder-fore to keep the engagement of the horse's inside hind, and straightness. *
*See Notes

Faults and Corrections

Faults that occur in competition, and suggested corrections are:

1) Haunches falling out. A possible cause is that the horse's outside hind lacks suppleness and strength, in which case it is back to the basics in longitudinal and lateral work in the trot and counter-canter, and riding many working pirouettes from renvers canter to the difficult side.

    Possible rider errors are: leaning the upper body too much to the inside; letting the outside rein cross over the horse's neck; insufficient driving aids, especially with the outside leg; poor preparation of the pirouette in the last strides.

2) Loss of bend. This can occur from lack of suppleness in the hind legs and shoulders. The best correction for this problem is to exercise the horse in shoulder-in and renvers in the trot, and shoulder-in at canter. Train working pirouettes on a 20 metre circle.

    Main rider errors are poor coordination of the aids and not preparing the pirouette properly in shoulder-fore in the last strides.

3) Over the bit. If a horse is over the bit in a pirouette, the chances are that he will show this fault in the other movements, such as transitions to the collected gaits, and in piaffe and passage. The problem can originate from poor conformation, such as a ewe neck, a thick jowl, and a weak or sore back. If this fault results from none of the above problems, there is a serious flaw in the horse's basic training.

    Main rider errors are improper position of the hands, over-collecting and poor preparation of the pirouette.

4) Loss of impulsion and rhythm. It is said that a true collected canter is really a four-beat canter, and that the naked eye is simply not fast enough to pick it up. I tend to agree with this statement. At any rate, in competition the collected canter must be ridden in three clean distinct beats, and the rhythm of the canter in the pirouette must remain the same. If pirouettes are overtrained and constantly ridden on the

spot, a horse will tire, and loss of impulsion and rhythm will occur.

5) Flat Pirouettes. These are executed in three or four strides pivoting around the horse's inside leg, with loss of rhythm and elevation. This fault can be caused by anticipation, or the rider's lack of knowledge and feel for, pirouettes. In most cases the rider tries to make the pirouette too tight on the spot.

Specific rider faults are overcollecting the last strides in shoulder-fore, too much use of the hands and insufficient driving aids with the legs, especially the inside leg. The rider may also lack feel, and intervene too late.

The other errors that often occur may all be attributed to the rider. They are:

i) Crossing over the line. In most cases this occurs when the rider fails to ride out of the pirouette early enough. With most horses it is necessary to ride straight out of the pirouette one stride early. The forward/sideways momentum of the horse will then put him on the line.

ii) Not performed on the line. When the first stride of the pirouette deviates to the outside of the line, it is always poor preparation and lack of outside rein and leg. As mentioned earlier, if the rider leans too much to the inside or crosses the outside rein over the horse's neck, this action does not help mobilize the haunches.

iii) Not at the marker. When the pirouette is started in front of the marker, it is usually due to the horse's anticipation, or the rider's lack of concentration. When I practise pirouettes on the diagonal or centre line in training, I always ride a few strides past the marker where the movement must be performed in competition. When the pirouette is executed past the marker, it is inevitably when the movement is started too late. With some horses you have to start the pirouette when their shoulders hit the marker and not wait for your knee and shoulder to reach it. Again, the first jump stride of the pirouette will bring the horse's body to the correct spot. This error of location can be often observed in the last pirouette at G in the Grand Prix Special, when sometimes not much room is left to perform a correct turn to the left at C.

As with everything else in life, common sense and practise must prevail; when an error occurs, you have to stop and think what went wrong and why. If there is a major flaw in the pirouette, it is unlikely that it will ever be corrected simply by practising pirouettes. You will have to analyse the problem and return to the basics to correct it. And lastly, but not least, it is very helpful to have a knowledgeable person on the ground to observe your work and render constructive criticism!

CHAPTER 30

~o~

Developing the Piaffe In Hand and Ridden

~o~

THE CORRECT PIAFFE IS AN ELEGANT, MAJESTIC, energetic, collected trot on the spot. The piaffe must at all times maintain the diagonal rhythm of the trot with increased cadence. The three joints of the hindquarters must flex evenly and the hindquarters must engage to the line of maximum lift, each bearing the same amount of weight. The hind legs must flex to allow the toes of the hooves to rise level with the middle, or top of the fetlocks. The hindquarters, thus bearing 90 per cent of the weight, liberate the forehand to rise, allowing the shoulders, in turn, to show great suppleness, and the forelegs to flex so that the forearms are approximately horizontal to the ground. The neck is raised by virtue of the great flexion of the hind legs and lifting of the shoulders. The poll must remain supple, the head engaged almost perpendicular to the ground. The cadence must be neither rushed nor slow. One must have the impression that the horse is always willing to move forward at any instant. Above all, the horse must remain soft and springy, not abrupt. The piaffe is, in essence, the cumulative result of years of training, and indeed its quality indicates failure or success at the highest levels of competition. Every horse can piaffe; but how?

Teaching In Hand

Conformation and temperament have a lot to do with the development of the piaffe, and to the time when training can be started. There is one cardinal rule, it must first be taught in hand.

Work in hand demands knowledge, experience and feel. I would advise any person desiring to perfect this technique not only to pay close attention to this chapter but, in addition, seek the help of a trainer with the proper credentials and years of experience. Work in hand, when properly performed, will produce excellent results, but incorrect training can have disastrous results.

PREPARATION AND EQUIPMENT

Horses can be started in hand with a long rein and an assistant holding it from behind, while the trainer remains at the point of the horse's shoulder holding the leading rein and whip. This

Rein set up for work in hand.

role can be interchanged with the trainer going back and working the long rein and whip, while the assistant holds the leading rein and helps keep the horse straight along the wall. I prefer to start horses in hand without long-reins and an assistant − primarily because this work is very delicate and I want total control of timing and feel.

Some trainers like to start work in hand with a cavesson over the snaffle, but I do not primarily because it causes loss of feel and timing. I therefore use the leading rein set in the Colbert position, that is, the leading rein run through the inside snaffle ring, over the poll and attached to the outside snaffle ring above the side rein and snaffle rein. The side reins must be set on the girth just under the buckles, or a little above the bottom of the saddle flaps and attached to the snaffle rings below the leading rein and above the snaffle reins. Minute attention to this adjustment is of the utmost importance, for the least little negative pressure on the snaffle can be very harmful. Careful attention to the adjustment of the side reins is also very important. You have to find an adjustment that will not hinder the horse's forward movement and yet restrain him enough so that he cannot run 'through' the leading rein.

The whip must be sufficiently long so that the trainer positioned at the point of the shoulder, or slightly in front, can reach the hindquarters without having to overstretch. The whip must be flexible, yet firm enough so that its action is quick yet light. However, the most important item is a pocket full of sugar cubes, or other such treats − more progress can be made with rewards than force! Finally, the trainer must be blessed with patience and understanding. Before going into exact details of work in hand, I would like to discuss the mounted preparation.

PREPARING THE HORSE

As peviously stated, conformation and temperament must determine when to start. A horse who is straight in the hindquarters will need a good deal of gymnastic training before he will be able to flex and engage his hindquarters. A horse with a hot temperament should not be worked in hand until his basic training gives him more maturity. As soon as the horse has reached sufficient lateral and longitudinal flexibility whereby he can perform good transitions and full halts in all gaits, I will proceed to work in hand, regardless of the horse's age. Logic dictates that lazy horses are best work in hand after a brief warm up, while their more highly-strung peers are best worked at the end of the mounted session. In the beginning of work in hand, I always prepare my horses with transitions; walk, trot, walk with no more than three or four strides of walk in between. This exercise will put the horse on the bit and bring up his back. I will then make a few full halts out of the trot, back into a strong lengthening in the trot, back into a full halt. This exercise will help animate the hindquarters. I then dismount along the wall on the left rein and have an assistant bring me the training reins, whip and sugar.

WORKING THE HORSE IN HAND

I set up, as previously explained, making sure to attach the side reins last. In case you have them adjusted too tight and the horse rears, it is best to be fully prepared with the leading rein. I pet the horse and pass my right hand over his left eye several times to assure him all is well. Now I start to teach the horse to walk forward and come back to a square halt absolutely parallel to the wall. I use my hand a little differently from the method considered classical: I raise it straight up on the leading rein to stop; I hold it back at the same level and angle as the reins would be if I were mounted, and I drop it straight down when in a neutral phase or when halted. Always positioned at the point of the horse's shoulder, I simply raise the whip near the horse's flanks to a position parallel to the ground, while at the same time I drop my hand down and back to the working position. If the horse fails to go forward, I tap him very lightly on the flank; when he moves forward, I immediately drop the whip so that the tip touches the ground, and pet and reward the horse with sugar. I stand on the spot for a few minutes and repeat the exercise until the horse moves forward the instant I raise the whip to the parallel position.

Once the horse learns to walk on in this manner, I start to teach him to trot on in the same way using the same aids, but naturally at first with a slightly firmer tap of the whip. If the horse becomes excited, the exercise must be stopped and the horse made to halt square until he has fully calmed down before the exercise can be started anew. In some instances when excitement builds to a point of fast breathing, the work should be stopped altogether for the day and the horse returned to his stable. A fight must be avoided at all costs. If the horse finds out how vulnerable the trainer is, it's all over bar the shouting and the trainer is the big loser. I would like to mention that I remove my spurs during the first days of work in hand. I am not as agile at running backwards as forwards, and I hate to trip on my spurs!

Once the horse walks and trots on willingly when you lift the whip without touching the flank, it is time to ask for a few little half steps forward. A half step is a half hoof, or hoof width forward. You simply raise the whip to ask for trot, but this time you restrain the horse more with the leading rein positioned back. If the horse does not respond, stop and try again, this time applying a few quick light taps of the whip slightly behind the haunch. Be satisfied with any sign of progress, stop and reward often. If you can get three half steps in trot rhythm, stop altogether for the day and return the horse to his stable.

Gradually, over a long period of time, the half steps will gain greater rhythm and cadence until a beginning of piaffe becomes apparent. At this time, I start working on the right rein. I have found that horses piaffe better to the right if they are dominant right, and since most are, this is a good rein to ask for a little more cadence. The only real reason to start to the left rein is that horses, by tradition, have been handled from their left sides. It is also a question of human dexterity; since most of us are dominant right, we are more adept at handling horses to their left or off sides. Work in hand must however, be continued to both reins, regardless.

When the horse piaffes without constant contact with the whip, it is time to ask for more collection and bending of the joints of the hind legs. If the horse does not respond to the whip on the flank and hip with increased effort, I then go after the hind legs with the whip using the following signals, which are a natural reflex for all horses: above the hocks on the thigh for forward impulsion; below the hocks on the metatarsus (cannon bone) for more engagement. It is very important to apply these whip aids only when the hind leg being touched is posed on the ground. I try not to overdo these whip aids, for I do not want the horse to become dependent on their signals to piaffe properly. At this stage, I do not concern myself with the forelegs; I only watch for any tendency they might have to cross. If this fault should begin to show, the half steps must be made more forward. I also avoid tapping the horse on top of the croup. While this action will activate the haunches, it tends to bring them up and eventually you could end up with a balancer (a swinging of the croup from side to side). During this work, it is important for the trainer to remain calm, very patient, but firm. The trainer must always remain positioned at the point of the horse's shoulders, and must not himself piaffe up and down while moving backward, but walk and run backward in quiet, positive steps. The use of the whip must be as conservative as possible, the positioning of the hands always correct, and their action firm, quick and light. Attention must always be paid to straightness, especially of the horse's neck and head. When working with one leading rein, the tendency, if one is not careful, is to pull the horse's head too much to the inside, which is very wrong. The trainer must ask for very little, but he must ask often for short periods; and reward often for very little effort. This work must be carried out every working day until obedience and acceptance are established. As the half steps develop into piaffe, it should not be asked for more than twice a week.

During these training stages, both in hand and ridden, the trainer must ensure that the horse does not engage his hind legs beyond the line of maximum lift, in order to maintain the even flexion of stifle, hock and fetlock. If the horse's hind legs engage too far in front of this optimum line, he will absorb more and more weight on his fetlocks and consequentially paralyse the action of hocks and stifles, which results in total loss of rhythm, cadence and tempo. It is for the same reason that the piaffe must not be shortened, or brought upon the spot, until the horse has gained optimum suppleness and strength and is able to flex the three joints of his hind legs to the maximum degree.

WORK IN HAND UNDER SADDLE

Once the horse can piaffe in hand almost on the spot, and his flexor extensors and gluteal muscles are well developed, it is time

Piaffe.

to put an assistant in the saddle and continue work in hand. It is important that the assistant remains very still in the saddle to allow the trainer to use the same signals as before, and to allow the horse to find his balance under the new weight. Once this process has been completed with success, it is time to continue to develop the piaffe ridden.

The Piaffe Ridden

THE AIDS

To ride the piaffe, some trainers prefer the use of the diagonal aids. Since the piaffe has a diagonal rhythm, these aids would seem to make sense. I have found however, that by use of diagonal aids, one can develop a pronounced balancer. I therefore use direct aids. Sometimes in the very beginning of training under saddle, the diagonal aids can help a horse gain better cadence, but as soon as this is achieved, I have found it wise to go back to direct aids. Also, it will help greatly if the leg aids are applied at the girth, rather than behind it. This sensitive area will promote the greatest response from a horse in both the piaffe and passage. In training the piaffe ridden, I do a lot of transitions from trot, to piaffe, back to trot, and from extended trot to piaffe, back to extended trot. Finally I ride from the walk to the piaffe, back to the walk. It is important, when transitioning from piaffe to walk, to keep the walk steps collected for a few strides. If the trainer rewards and gives the horse a long rein and walks off in a free walk, it will be more difficult later on to teach the transitions piaffe, passage, piaffe.

DEALING WITH FAULTS

There are several faults that can occur during this phase of training. A horse can resist by bringing his haunches to the inside, or becoming too stiff in his poll and over the bit. I correct this fault by riding the exercise in shoulder-fore, or if necessary, in shoulder-in on three tracks. A horse can show irregular steps, or outright lack of engagement of a hind leg. When this occurs, I train the piaffe in shoulder-in on a 10 metre circle. For instance, if a horse shows lack of engagement of the right hind, I put him on a circle left and ask for piaffe in shoulder-in left. This will stretch the outside right lateral as much as possible, and in a short time the horse will become even. A horse can piaffe wide behind; if this occurs, the exercise must be trained more forward with many energetic transitions to trot and back. With such horses, the trainer should not ask for too much cadence and elevation − it is best to move on and perfect the passage, after which stage the horse will be stronger and better able to find his self-carriage, cadence and elevation. Horses who rear in the piaffe usually use this defence for one or more of the following reasons: poor or brutal training methods in the initial development of the exercise; being asked to piaffe on the spot too soon; overtraining of the piaffe; use of strong, awkward aids on the part of the rider, or a genuine physical problem in the hind-quarters. It is always wise to consult a veterinarian to find out if there is an overriding problem, and correct it whenever possible.

Whatever the reason for rearing, the best corrective action is to stop training piaffe altogether for several months. After a time, the trainer can ask for short periods of passage once or twice a week, outside and on the return to the stable. Once the horse agrees willingly, and above all, happily, to passage outside, the trainer can start to ask for shorter and shorter steps in the passage until the horse can perform a few steps of passage on the spot. If the horse shows any tendency to rear, he must be ridden forward in the strong trot and all further demands stopped until the next training session. Finally, when the horse can passage on the spot in open country, he can be brought back to the dressage arena and gradually asked to passage, and eventually made to shorten his strides until two or three are obtained in the spot. The shortening of the passage steps must be asked for on a circle, or at the corners of the arena; never on straight lines, or the centre line.

PERFECTING TRAINING

Once this training has been perfected, it is time to ask the horse to piaffe on the centre line, and at first in half steps forward, never on the spot; except in the actual dressage tests where it is required. Some horses have a problem finding their balance on the spot, and in most cases this problem can be overcome by practising the piaffe on a circle. This problem often arises with horses that overflex and engage their hind legs far in front of the line of maximum lift in an effort to relieve their hocks and absorb most of their weight on the fetlocks. The circle helps the horse come back on the spot without losing impulsion or rhythm, for he feels that if he cannot piaffe forward, he can shift some of his weight sideways. Eventually, he should find his balance on a straight line and on the spot. In certain difficult cases, when the circle is not a means to an end, it is best to perfect the passage to further strengthen the hindquarters, and eventually return to the piaffe on a small circle out of the passage. If the horse still has difficulty finding his balance on the spot at this stage of training, I have found that coming down from the passage and asking for the piaffe in a pirouette is helpful. While in the pirouette, say to the right, I simply restrain the sideward steps with both legs and outside rein until I obtain a few steps on the spot. As soon as I feel an imminent loss of impulsion and cadence, I move sideways again and repeat. When the horse can maintain cadence in a pirouette right, I start the same exercise to the left. When the horse is proficient to the left, I alternate directions in the pirouette, then, while in a pirouette right, I restrain and ask for two or three steps on the spot and immediately reverse to the left and repeat. The change of direction and shifting of weight helps refine the ultimate balance and cadence on the spot.

Finally, the piaffe can be a victim of conformation. A short-coupled horse will always be able to show more elevation and bring his forearms to the vertical, while a long-coupled horse will find it more difficult, and indeed may never be able to show the same brilliance. Horses with weak hindquarters will never be able to maintain the high degree of cadence required for the correct piaffe.

One must have a sound theatrical knowledge, patience and highly developed feel for equestrian tact. Only with these assets, can one successfully train a horse to his utmost in the piaffe. When properly trained and presented, the piaffe brings out the ultimate beauty and athleticism in a horse. It is the exercise that dictates success or failure at the highest level of competition, and brings about the ultimate expression of art.

Guérinière's definition fo the piaffe is:

> When a horse passages in place without advancing, backing or traversing itself, and when it lifts and bends its forearms high and in good grace, we call this step, piaffer. This gait, which is very noble was much sought after on the parade grounds and at festivals on horseback: it is still very much esteemed in Spain; the horses of that country and the Neapolitans, show much aptitude.

The definition of *piaffer* in the French dictionary is: 'To paw the ground, to fidget, to fume.' It would seem that the authors attended a good many dressage compteitions!*
*See Notes.

CHAPTER 31

—o—

Passage

—o—

T HE CORRECT PASSAGE, LIKE THE PIAFFE, IS A SLOW, majestic highly cadenced trot. It has the same long moment of suspension between the posing of the diagonal pair of legs. The horse's hind hooves engage to the line of maximum lift, and, with equal distribution of weight, flex to a point slightly above the fetlocks and propel the horse powerfully forward and upward. The haunches, thus lowered and engaged, carry approximately 60 per cent of the weight, allowing the shoulders to rise and show great suppleness and expression. The horse's neck is raised, the poll remaining the highest point, and the head is flexed almost perpendicular to the ground. The horse's forelegs flex sufficiently to allow the forearms to rise parallel to the ground.

Over the years, there has been a good deal of controversy over passage and piaffe. The French school advocated that piaffe was nothing more than passage on the spot. The German school maintained that the piaffe was a highly collected, cadenced, rhythmic trot on the spot; and indeed the F.E.I. has also supported this definition, There is basically no differenece between the two schools of thought; it is simply a question of upward thrust and cadence. In training the piaffe, or in warming up in this exercise, we allow the upward thrust to move forward in half steps, maintaining rhythm and cadence. When the horse has attained sufficient strength and suppleness in his back and hindquarters,

Passage.

we can mobilize this power on the spot – this is piaffe. In the passage, we deliberately create this upward thrust and convert it into forward floating steps.* What we see so often in competition are transitions into piaffe, where the exercise loses its thrust, cadence, and rhythm and becomes nothing more than a flat trot on the spot, or 'chicken scratching'. This type of piaffe belongs to neither school – although some may call it trot on the spot! To be correct and classical, the thrust, cadence and rhythm of both movements must remain identical.

*See Notes.

Teaching the Horse

The passage is the last upper level exercise I teach a horse. While the piaffe can be started earlier in hand, the passage should be trained ridden, and demands that the horse achieve perfect straightness and balance before training can commence. However, in certain cases where a horse has great natural cadence in the trot, he can be taught the passage before the piaffe. In such cases, the trainer may gradually shorten the passage steps — gaining in height what is lost in length — and, by the increased flexion of the stifles, hocks and fetlocks, lower the croup without losing the rhythm of the passage, and piaffe on the spot.

The passage may be trained out of the piaffe, or the collected trot. It is a matter of temperament, the degree of training, and the horse's natural ability to piaffe. In order to teach a horse to passage out of the piaffe, the piaffe must be trained in its final finished form on the spot in order to develop a correct passage. If the piaffe is not perfected, I teach my horses the passage out of the collected trot, and eventually I mould the passage and piaffe into one continual rhythmic expression. The advantages of teaching the passage out of the trot are that its training can be started sooner and, if you run into difficulties in balancing the piaffe on the spot, piaffe training can be stopped and the passage further developed to strengthen the horse's back and hindquarters before returning to piaffe again.

When training passage out of piaffe, you simply drive the horse to piaffe out of the collected walk and gradually increase leg, seat and back pressure until the horse converts his upward thrust into forward floating rhythmic steps.

When starting out of the collected trot, more preparation is needed. First I ask the horse for many transitions from the extended trot to collected trot, and gradually diminish the number of extended and collected steps. When the horse is very light to my legs and hands, and is well balanced under my seat, I ask for a few strong trot steps and almost immediately restrain the forward motion by increasing my driving aids and restraining the forward movement with my hands. After a few tries, most horses will offer a stride or two of passage steps. I then stop, reward, and start again. In a short time, the horse will offer as many passage steps as he can physically give. It is important not to ask for too much too soon!

In the beginning of passage training, I do not ask for piaffe steps on the days I train passage, and vice versa. When the horse can passage with perfect regularity, I start to mould the exercises into one, through transitions. The transition piaffe – passage is relatively simple; while in the piaffe, increase your driving aids until you convert the upward thrust into forward floating steps. The rider's hands must restrain the forward movement enough to maintain high collection. It is better to raise the hands slightly, rather than pull backward.

The transition passage – piaffe is more delicate and calls for the utmost equestrian tact. You have to shorten the passage steps very gradually without losing height, rhythm, thrust and cadence until the horse can be brought on the spot without any loss of balance. In the beginning of training this transition, it is wise not to bring the horse completely on the spot, but to allow the horse a few half steps forward until he feels comfortable in his balance on the spot.

I have been told Otto Loerke once stated: 'The only time I ask a horse to piaffe on the spot is on Sunday morning before church when I can confess this sin!' The F.E.I. has, over the years, decreased and increased the difficulty of the Grand Prix test to meet the current standard. It has, however, never allowed half steps forward in the Grand Prix. Therefore, as trainers and competitors, we must make sure that our horses attain the greatest degree of suppleness and strength possible in the back and hindquarters in order to be able to perform the piaffe on the spot when it is called for. I agree with Loerke's statement – it is not a good idea to train piaffe on the spot too often. Just as canter pirouettes should not always be ridden on the spot all the time, these two movements must be trained and exercised in their working form in order not to put undue stress on the hindquarters.

When I first start teaching the passage, I ask and settle for a 'soft passage' that maintains rhythm and cadence without the greater thrust eventually needed to become a true passage. As the horse becomes stronger and more supple, I increase my demands until I obtain the maximum upward forward thrust.

Faults and Corrections in Training

The same faults that show up in the piaffe can creep into the passage:

1) Dragging hind legs. Horses who show this fault have not reached sufficient suppleness and strength in their basic training and are not ready.
2) Stiff back. Horses who show stiff backs in the passage are in essence performing a hovering tense trot. If this fault is only a temporary problem, it can be corrected by riding forward in an extended trot and then coming back into the passage. You can also ride a few long half-passes in the trot across the diagonals of the riding hall. If this problem persists, then it is wise to go back to the basics, or in severe cases, to consult a veterinarian for possible problems in the hindquarters or back.
3) Balancer, wide behind, and crossing front legs. These faults usually all originate from stiffness in the back and hindquarters, or outright bad training. They can best be corrected by riding forward and practising many transitions; collected trot, passage, collected trot.
4) Irregular steps. The short engagement of a hind leg in the passage can be caused by rider error – the rider not sitting absolutely correctly with equal weight on both seat bones, or using one leg with more strength. When irregular steps are not caused by rider faults, they most often originate from a stiffness, or weakness in the hindquarters. The best way to remedy this problem is to ride the passage in shoulder-in to the opposite side of the short steps, in order to stretch the outside lateral forward as much as possible. This correction must be made on straight lines, for in the passage, it is important to keep the horse straight to allow the hindquarters to track forward in line with the front legs; only when the

horse is tracking on two tracks can you develop correct forward thrust. In the piaffe, we can place the horse in shoulder-in on a circle to correct the same problem in a hind leg and still develop upward thrust, but in the passage we must stay on straight lines in the beginning of training in order to develop correct straight forward thrust. If this fault persists, the use of a whip should be attempted. The rider simply taps the horse on his flank on the short side, at the exact moment that the short-stepping hoof touches the ground. This will promote upward and forward movement of that hind leg. The use of the whip must not be overdone or the horse will only passage correctly when whip aids are applied. Irregular steps can also be caused by the horse's lack of balance. In such cases, persistent short training sessions in piaffe and passage over a long period will eventually correct this problem.

Whenever I run into problems training the passage, I take the horse cross-country and ask for the exercise out of the collected trot on my return to the stable when the horse's natural impulsion is at its maximum. This allows the rider to use the horse's natural strength against the horse without any effort.

Transition Faults in Competition

Other faults which most often occur in the passage, and mostly in the Grand Prix and Grand Prix Special tests, are the transitions into the passage, and from the passage to collected canter.

The transition collected walk — passage must be straight, forward and clear. There must be no short piaffe steps, nor short, shuffling trot steps. The rider must make sure that the horse is well on the bit in the collected walk, and bring the horse lower on the bit in the last few walk strides in order not to allow the horse to come up over the rider's hands and block his back in the transitional step. If the horse tends to perform the transition by use of a few half steps forward, the rider must think 'collected trot' at the moment the passage is asked for. The transition collected trot to passage, must also be ridden with the horse lower than normal in the last trot strides to assure that he cannot come up over the bit, and stiffen his back. In the transition extended trot to passage, the rider must assure that there is no loss of impulsion in the last strides of the extended trot. If there is a loss of tempo and impulsion, the transition to passage will be late, lazy or will eventually only develop out of collected trot steps.

The transition from passage to the collected canter is almost always a problem of anticipation, since most horses are eager to abandon these majestic steps for the easier collected canter. This can easily be handled by never asking for the canter depart in practise where it is called for in the test, but to ride well past the marker and only then ask for the transition. In this transition, the rider must also sit very softly in the saddle and ask for the canter depart with a very steady inside leg at the girth.

This transition in the Grand Prix Special is somewhat different. Here, the horse is asked to turn to the right across the short side, and when reaching the centre line of the arena, to canter on his left lead. The natural reflex for all horses, when turned to a side, is to expect the canter depart to the same side as the turn. Therefore, in this transition in the Special, the rider must hold the horse a little more with the outside (right) leg to mobilize the haunches and demand the strike-off left with the inside (left) leg at the girth. Also, in this transition, it is wise to practise the canter depart left well after the horse has crossed the centre line of the arena to avoid any eventual anticipation during the actual test.

CHAPTER 32

Nervous And
Headstrong Horses

THROUGHOUT MY LIFE I HAVE ALWAYS PREFERRED HIGHLY strung horses. I have found them to be highly talented for the highest levels of competition, good friends, and more intelligent than their quieter peers. In essence, they have a touch of class. I wish I could say the same for some humans I have known with the same qualities! The training of such athletes has, by necessity, to vary in intensity and method. One of the most enlightening and helpful exercises I have ever practiced with such horses came from the German master Oskar Stensbeck, who used to train nervous and headstrong horses by riding into the riding hall, halting in the centre of the hall, and letting his horse chew the bit progressively from his hand. He would then light a cigar and read his newspaper until the cigar was burnt out. During this time, he would never let the horse move out of the square halt. He would then dismount after this meditation exercise for the horse, and return him to the stable. This exercise is not only good in disciplining and calming an agitated horse, but it also teaches the animal to balance the rider's weight by using his own forces — the first step to self-carriage. I no longer smoke and I doubt I could do much justice to a newspaper while mounted. However, whenever I have a busy teaching schedule, I make sure that I have my most nervous horse to sit on in the middle of the hall, on long reins, in a perfect square halt — it works wonderfully.

Preparation Before Work

Needless to say, I turn all my young horses out to pasture whenever possible. However, as they become more experienced and valuable, I do not let them outside, for fear of accident. They get their day of play free-jumping in the indoor hall.

I do not adhere to cutting back on feed (although trying different types of feed that might have a calming effect is wise). Neither do I advocate using tranquillizers, or such tricks as leaving them unblanketed overnight outdoors to freeze, so that they are sapped of energy the next day. Such methods may work to solve the immediate problem, but they will have devastating long term effects.

Frequent lungeing before mounted work is always helpful, however, too much lungeing can be harmful. Long sessions on the lunge line tend to make the horse fitter and fitter, which makes a nervous horse even harder to calm. Overuse of the lunge line also puts undue stress and torque on the horse's joints. Therefore, lungeing, while an invaluable exercise, must be practiced with caution and moderation.

Another method I often use is letting the horse, under full tack, with the reins crossed over the saddle and under the stirrup leathers, run free in the riding hall until he is rid of his pent-up energy and sufficiently calm and settled to start mounted work. This method is quicker than lungeing and eliminates a long period of warming up when mounted.

Training

My training programme with highly strung horses always includes more collected than extended work in the beginning of training, and long walk periods on a long rein between exercises. In essence I will work such horses less intensively, but for a longer period of time.

I have found that shoulder-in, followed by a circle back into shoulder-in and diminishing circles in the trot are effective exercises in the beginning. When the horse is relaxed in the trot, I will ask for lengthenings down the long side, and transitions back to working trot, with circles of 10−8 metres on the short sides. If the horse is too 'hot' to lengthen in the rising trot, I simply sit the lengthenings until he is sufficiently relaxed. At that point, I will start lengthening the stride in the rising trot on the long sides of the hall, and finally across the diagonals, making sure to keep the horse very straight on the diagonals, not letting his haunches sway out in the downward transition approaching the wall.

Working over properly spaced cavalletti (not too long a stride) is always a good method of relaxing a nervous horse, while at the same time building suppleness, musculature and cadence.

I do not attempt to canter a nervous horse until he is fully settled in the trot on circles, shoulder-in, lengthenings, transitions, half-halts and full halts. At this stage, I will ask the horse to canter on his easier lead (usually the left) on a 20 metre circle. When the horse canters well balanced, without resistance, and in proper bend on both reins, I ask for 10 metre circles within the 20 metre circle to both reins, changing direction through the circle with simple changes of lead through the trot. I then take the horse large with 10 metre circles (bigger with some horses) on the short sides of the hall. If the horse remains calm at this stage, I start working the diagonals with trot transitions at X and canter departs to the new lead when reaching the long sides. If the horse becomes unsettled I go back to the 20 metre circle and ask for transitions canter − trot − canter on both reins until the horse settles and can be returned to the diagonals.

Working Outdoors

When the horse becomes sufficiently routined and calm in these basic exercises in trot and canter, I will start his training cross-country. In the beginning, I will relax the horse first in the riding hall, and then I will go cross-country for a long walk. I always choose days that are not too cold, or windy. If a very quiet horse is available to accompany me, a companion can only add to the pleasure. Sometimes I have found that stopping in a meadow and letting the horse stretch and graze for periods of time is very helpful. I never attempt to trot or canter until the horse is fully relaxed in the walk. At that stage a slow progression of cross-country work can start.

On occasion, I have had highly strung horses who were very difficult to settle down outdoors under any conditions. With such horses, I have found that lungeing them on a steep incline is very conducive to settling their excess adrenalin. The important thing here is to adjust the side reins loosely enough to allow the horse to stretch his neck fully; to use a lungeing cavesson; and to lunge on as large a circle as possible. Also, contrary to normal lungeing principles, the trainer must accompany the horse a little up and down the incline in order to reduce undue torque and stress on the horse's joints. I always strive to start the horse out in the working trot, but if he wants to canter, so be it. Eventually he will stretch his neck forward and downward in the canter uphill, and collect himself in the trot downhill until he tires and falls into the walk. When this occurs, I continue to lunge in the walk until the horse's breathing is back to normal. Very soon the horse will trot and canter at will on the incline on both reins. This exercise not only calms a horse very quickly, but also develops very good musculature over all parts of the body. It is, incidentally, excellent for improving a poor walk. When the horse walks down a steep incline, his hip joints swing farther forward than on the flat. This helps develop better overtracking. However, a little bit goes a long way – this is a very strenuous exercise for a horse and extreme caution is recommended.

When Things Go Wrong

Whenever there is retrogression in the training of a highly strung, nervous horse, or something goes wrong during a training session, my cardinal rule is to go back to the square halt, and let the horse stand on the spot, chewing the bit from my hands. When the horse has become docile again, I finish the session by walking on a long rein. If you get mentally worn out by the overabundance of patience required, just think of how easy the training of piaffe and passage will be...

CHAPTER 33

~⊙~

Riding Cross-Country

~⊙~

WHENEVER THE WEATHER AND FOOTING PERMIT, I can be found training outside. I have discovered over the years that horses stay fresher, more alert, and in general progress faster in their training cross-country. The changing conditions and increased flow of adrenalin help.

I also make good use of the terrain — hills, slopes and straight flat areas. I use the angle of the terrain to place the horse in the desired balance and position. For instance, it is easier to collect the trot downhill, where the hocks are naturally placed farther under by virtue of the incline. A horse in this position can be trained in half steps forward in piaffe. On the other hand, I will extend the trot going uphill, where the horse's haunches are below his shoulders. The incline, in this case, will force the horse to drive more with his hocks and liberate his shoulders, and stretch his neck downward for more reach. Horses who need to develop more length of stride in the walk can be improved by walking down steep inclines on a loose rein; this will allow the hip joints to swing forward to their maximum flexibility. The reason for walking downhill to increase stride length whilst trotting downhill to assist collection is as follows. In the walk, very little kinetic energy is produced, and the horse does not have to brace his back muscles as much as in trot and canter, and is thus freer of tension and able to swing his hind legs forward. The incline transfers weight to the forehand and increases his

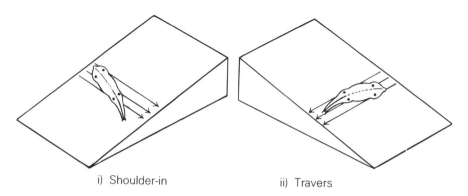

i) Shoulder-in   ii) Travers

Using natural slopes for remedial work on shoulder-in and travers.

ability to stretch hind legs forward for greater overtracking.

Slopes can be used for lateral work. For instance, a horse who is very strong and convex on his right side can be worked in shoulder- in right, on a left to right (uphill) slope. The angle of the terrain will make it easier for the horse to oscillate his right hind leg under and forward while lifting the right shoulder and lowering the left, thus helping the bend. Travers with such horses will also be facilitated on a left to right incline. Here, the weight of the hindquarters will more readily pass over and flex the inside hind, helping right lateral bend.

The large flat areas are most useful for work in the canter. Here it is useful to pick a tree, or other object in the distance, in order to establish a straight line. Sometimes a mower will leave adequate lines to follow. I like to practise flying changes and zigzags in the canter under these conditions where I can ride on indefinitely without limitations of space. The important thing is to establish a straight line so that the changes are straight and the zigzags even to both sides. Horses with four-beat canters can improve by cantering on varied terrain to enhance natural balance. The only time I will canter a horse on steep hills is when I wish to improve his conditioning or strengthen his abdominal muscles. Natural obstacles, such as ditches and tree trunks, can be jumped in the trot to improve longitudinal flexibility. Piaffe and passage can be practised on the return to the stable when natural impulsion will be at its highest level. It is a pity farmers get so upset when they find fresh hoofprints in their fields! Dry, light plough is excellent footing to improve the cadence of the trot. Hay fields or the like are excellent places to go for long straight trots to strengthen loose or weak stifles.

Mother nature offers unlimited possibilities. It is up to the rider's imagination to think, explore, and use the endless opportunities the terrain gives to work a horse, above all, to make it enjoyable for the horse. The rider, also, should relax and enjoy the unlimited beauty to be discovered in the countryside. As the great golfer Walter Hagen once said: 'You're only here for a short visit. Don't hurry. Don't worry. And be sure to smell the flowers along the way.'

CHAPTER 34

―○―

Preparing For Competition

―○―

THE RIDER'S AND HORSE'S ULTIMATE SUCCESS OR failure in competition starts from the very first day of training. If the rider has developed a classic seat, has been trained to execute all movements and exercises with great accuracy at all times and has a relaxed, disciplined mind which can concentrate on the task at hand as well as think for the horse, success will be more easily attained. A rider with a classic seat can develop feel and, by correct daily training, the mind will develop accuracy and precision. In essence, we can say that feel plus mind equals equestrian tact. Without this ultimate refinement, success in competition will be very difficult to achieve. Riders who have not been trained to ride correctly have short careers in the competition arena. They may enjoy success with one horse, but they do not succeed with a variety of horses.

The Training Schedule

―○―

The training schedule must be well thought out and the work intelligently planned so that horse and rider reach their peaks at the right moment. Each horse requires different preparation, and it is up to the trainer to find the right approach. Over the years I have observed that most riders tend to get more and more uptight as the competition day nears, especially before Championships and Olympic Games. They tend to overwork their horses and drill the weak movements. While this is human nature at work, it can, nevertheless, have catastrophic results. These horses will most often 'sour out' and not be at the top of their form on the big day. Each horse has his own personality in the competition arena. Some of the main problems are laziness, hot temper, anticipation and horses becoming ring wise.

Horses who are lazy by nature will never achieve greatness at the higher levels. Whenever I have to train a lazy horse, I ride him as much as possible cross-country and rest the horse on long walks before competition. You simply have to get such horses rested in order to muster as much spark as possible.

Horses full of fire require the rider's utmost time and patience. I have found that very slow, long warm-ups help. If you lunge and overwork such horses in an effort to quieten them down, you simply make them fitter and fitter until you reach the point of overstressing their bodies and minds. With a spirited horse, I usually start my work in the working walk, performing lateral and longitudinal exercises, and gradually take up the same exercises in the working trot. I do not ask for any highly collected movements until the horse is completely relaxed and on my aids. Long slow work cross-country can be very beneficial before competition. Slow work twice a day will always be helpful, providing you do not overdo it.

Horses who anticipate are usually the seasoned veterans, or the horses who are overdrilled in practising tests. In either case, the solution is easy; stop riding the tests. When work on the test becomes necessary, ride the movements out of sequence.

Horses who become ring wise can be a real problem. If a long rest away from competition and relaxed cross-country training fail, I know nothing other than harsh punishment administered in the actual arena while riding *hors concours* at a small show. When I have to contend with a lazy horse, or a horse who is ring wise, I always train such horses with dull spurs and revert to sharp spurs to ride the test. This tactic can make life easier. Finally, it is through actual competitive conditions that one really gets to know a horse. This knowledge will give

the exact information needed to devise the right warm-up programme for that individual.

Travel, Preparation and Team Work

Consideration must also be given to the horse's ability to travel
and, in the case of international competition, the location. If a
horse is a bad shipper, logic dictates that you arrive at the
competition site as early as possible. In the case of international
competition, one can be called to perform at high altitude and
across oceans. In either case, you have two choices: arrive the
day before and go for it, or arrive one month ahead of time to let
the horse acclimatize. When going for the first option, it is wise
to take enough food and water to last the horse throughout the
competition.

Another rule to proper preparation is: 'Never leave home
without it'. You do not want to arrive at the show to find out
that someone forgot to pack the boot jack, or bridle. One should
have a master packing list and diligently go over it in minute
detail prior to leaving. I once had a student who was so scatter-
brained she took off with her trailer forgetting to load her horse!

Finally, proper ground management is essential. There must
be perfect team play between groom, trainer and rider; time
scheduled for feeding, watering, grooming and warm-up established and adhered to. Efforts must be made by everyone to
remain calm, collected and happy under stress.

Mental Preparation of the Rider

When I first started to compete in international horse shows, I
was very nervous. In fact, I found it hard to sleep the night
before, and usually lost my appetite. These factors did not help
me and made me overly tired when I had to perform. The only
solutions I can offer for this problem are the ones I tried with
moderate success – go out the night before, have fun, drink a

few beers, then go to bed and sleep soundly for a few hours – or go to bed early with someone of voracious sexual appetites!

Seriously though, as one gains competitive experience, the nerves subside. As a matter of fact, after twenty years entering and exiting dressage arenas, I find it hard to get myself mentally 'up', and this can be just as bad as being too nervous. To ride well in competition, it is essential to have a little edge. Another mental factor to contend with at these early stages is fear of forgetting the test. To counter this before an important event I find a quiet spot, sit in my captain chair, close my eyes, block my mind to the outside world, and, in deep, slow concentration, ride every step of the test as though I were on the horse right down to the last halt and salute. Instead of memorizing the test marker to marker in the arena, I concentrate on putting all the movements of the test in their proper context. This thought process is faster and helps save the day if, for some reason, one has a lapse of memory during the performance.

Last, but not least, make plans to enjoy the horse show. Have dinner with friends, visit interesting local places, or indeed do whatever turns you on. It is important not to forget that you are riding for your personal pleasure and fun, so make sure that you have an enjoyable time.

CHAPTER 35

~―o―~

Warming Up

~―o―~

E VERY HORSE WARMS UP DIFFERENTLY DEPENDING ON his age, degree of training, and temperament. There are, however, two cardinal rules that I adhere to:

1) The horse's dominant lateral must always be stretched and suppled first.
2) The horse must obtain his maximum possible lateral flexibility and oscillation of the hind legs before longitudinal transitions and suppleness can be obtained.

Approaches for Different Horses

~―o―~

Young horses are best warmed up in the rising trot with low neck carriage, but enough flexion in the poll to bring up their backs, and sufficient driving aids to sustain the engagement of their hindquarters. The horse must be kept united for best gymnastic results. The rider should rise on the horse's weak diagonal to strengthen the weaker lateral and start on large circles to the left if the horse is dominant right, or vice versa.

Older and advanced horses are best started in their warm-ups in the walk in voltes, shoulder-in, renvers and half-passes. The walk allows the horse to stretch his legs laterally to their maximum, thus suppling the adductors and abductors of the legs as well as all the dorsal muscles. In the two-beat rhythm of the trot, the horse passes from one diagonal to the other, and during this time of suspension between the diagonal transfer, the horse is robbed of the complete crossing of his legs because the leg being crossed disengages itself a fraction of a second prematurely. The warm-up in the walk in lateral exercises also helps put the horse on the aids and is very helpful to quieten a nervous horse when just mounted.

When the horse is supple and on the aids in walk, I start the same lateral exercises in trot. As soon as the horse is supple and yielding, I move on to longitudinal suppling, which is attained by all transitions and reaches its highest degree of perfection in the transition extended trot − piaffe − extended trot.

Once the horse is supple, round and light to my aids in the trot, I start to canter on the horse's better lead (usually the left). I canter in shoulder-fore down the long sides to promote the engagement of the inside hind leg and straightness. On the short sides, I ride circles. The size of the circles depends on the horse's age and degree of training. They vary from 15 to 6 metres in diameter. I will then ask for several lengthenings of stride still in shoulder-fore on both reins. At this stage, I will stop and rest the horse in the free walk on a long rein before starting whatever it is I plan to work on that given day.

Horses with physical problems can sometimes be better warmed up with different approaches. For instance, horses with ewe necks or thick jowls, can best be warmed up and put on the bit on the working trot on circles of 15 to 20 metres with many transitions trot − canter − trot. Horses with long backs who still tend to work 'in two pieces' and are still reluctant to use their hindquarters, can best be warmed up initially in little half steps forward in the piaffe. Lazy horses and horses with a poor trot can best be warmed up in the canter. The natural three-beat rhythm of the canter stride creates impulsion and will wake up a phlegmatic horse. A cold-backed horse should be warmed up on the lunge line before being mounted. I always try to keep my warm-ups to a minimum to conserve the horse's energy for the lesson of the day.

Learning From Experience

Warming up for competition can be very different from the daily routines. The rider must be very familiar with the horse's composure in public and his reaction in unfamiliar places and objects.

Since experience is the best teacher, let me narrate my two warm-ups in the 1975 Pan American games in Mexico City which turned out to be hard lessons. My mount, Leopardi, was always a difficult horse in the competition arena. Leopardi's brilliance could be explosive, while his resilience had a short span and, when this was exceeded, his mind became one track toward the stable! To warm up such a horse was always a challenge.

The first competition was the Grand Prix team competition. Since I was the anchorman for our team, my thoughts were to ride a conservative test and not set Mexico on fire. Just before I started to warm up, our coach, the late Bengt LJunquist, confirmed to me that my teammates Hilda Gurney, on Keen, and Dorothy Morkis, on Monaco, had done well and that I had to score 1386 points for the team to win. This only made me more conservative in my thoughts. Contrary to the golden rule, with Leopardi, I overworked him in the warm-up to make sure that he would not explode in the ring and jeopardize the team's chances. When it was my turn to enter, I approached the entrance gate and Leopardi reared straight up and refused point-blank to enter. After a short fight, which was proving futile, I dismounted and led Leopardi into the enclosure on foot! Thank goodness Frank Chapot and my friend, Evie Thorndike, were right behind me. The bell was ringing and I knew I had only two minutes to enter the ring. Frank and Evie helped me mount. I gathered my composure, didn't waste any time, cantered off on the right lead and didn't blink until halted at X. Leopardi did not have the resilience he needed to be brilliant; in fact he felt tired. He did not, however, let me down. Our only mistake came toward the end of the test where he missed the eleventh change every stride; a real sign of fatigue for him . After my final halt, I was, on one hand, relieved that we had got through the test, and on the other, I was mad at myself for overworking Leopardi in the warm-up, which put him on the dull side, and almost soured out. I was the last rider to go, so I did not dismount outside – another mistake, because everyone came running, and I was surrounded by a sea of humans. Leo and I both wanted out, but there was no place to flee... My score was announced, 1683 points. Our team had won the gold medal for the United States! I still reminded myself later how that warm-up had brought us dangerously near disaster.

The next day, we competed for the individual championship. In the Grand Prix Special, I always feel more relaxed – there is not as much pressure as in the team championship. After all, if you do not do well, you make almost every other rider happy! In view of the previous day, and considering the great demands of the piaffe and passage in the Special, I decided to give Leopardi a very short warm-up. This time Leopardi was eager to enter the enclosure and we trotted around the arena, doing a few transitions. Leo's back was up and strong, his ears set forward; he was floating! I thought everything was right for an individual gold. My hopes were soon shattered. After my halt at X, I proceeded in collected trot to C and turned left. At the same moment, the judge at H lost all his score sheets to a gust of wind. To make matters worse, he lowered his big straw hat in a violent gesture in an effort to retrieve his papers. Needless to say, Leopardi bolted and never again settled down throughout the test. The only way I could ride him through the corner at H was in shoulder-in! We ended up in fourth place with a score of 64.46 per cent. If I had warmed Leopardi up in his normal routine, he would have shied in the corner by H; but he would have settled down throughout the remainder of the test. However, with the very powerful little word 'if', I could have put all of Mexico in a bottle! The mistakes I made in these two warm-ups surely made me more aware of how important the proper thinking, planning and executing a warm up can be; not having to fantasize about the little conjunction 'if'.

CHAPTER 36

Competition

NATIONAL COMPETITIONS SERVE TO PREPARE YOUNG horses
for international tournaments, to develop novice riders, and
to provide good sport for the horses and riders who cannot or
do not wish to compete at the highest levels of dressage. Rules,
guidelines, and tests are developed and regulated by the National
Federations of each country. Since almost every National Federation is a member of the Federation Equestre Internationale (the
international governing body of equestrian sport), the rules and
guidelines are very similar. The national tests, however, vary
from country to country and therefore, a closer look at the
national scene is necessary.*

National Competitions

Rules are rules whether we like them or not. As competitors, we
have to accept them in good faith and live by them. Guidelines,
however, can only give students, competitors and trainers a
general idea of how to train horses up through the levels. For-
tunately, every horse is different. Therefore, his training must
progress to suit his individual needs, and guidelines should not
be considered inviolate. Tests serve as checkpoints to see how
the horse's training is progressing, and are helpful to school and
develop horses under actual competitive situations. The rewards

*See Notes.

they offer give the competitors goals to achieve. American national tests are, by and large, theoretically sound. There are, however, several exercises incorporated in them which can be harmful to the young horse: leg-yielding at the trot, collected walk before the horse is sufficiently supple and strong and rein-back before the horse has achieved sufficient longitudinal suppleness.

National awards can prove to be harmful to rider, horse and sport if they are based on 'point chasing'. This procedure has nothing to do with proper gymnastic development of the horse, and is only a misleading ego trip for the competitor. Some poor riders will keep their horses for years at the same level of competition and, through drilling and repetition, end up with dull winning-machines at secondary level. Such forms of competition have nothing to do with sport or art. Furthermore, a knowledgeable trainer will not have to proceed national level by level to reach international standards. Rather, he will use his intellect and experience to develop horses systematically and classically using only levels and tests as needed in the process of developing a true champion.

International Competitions

International competitions are held under the auspices of the F.E.I., which is responsible for legislation, regulation and composing the international tests to be ridden in all international competitions. By and large, the F.E.I. tests are fair and well received by competitors with, perhaps, the exception of the Intermediate II test, which for many years has proved unpopular, regardless of the revisions and changes which have been made. The Grand Prix and Grand Prix Special tests are the two tests that tower over the discipline as the highest pinnacle that can be reached in competitive dressage.

Every four years, the F.E.I. revise their tests to meet the changing standard of world dressage. The tests vary little in difficulty. Great emphasis is always placed on piaffe and passage and their transitions. The main drawbacks to international competition are encompassed in judging, nationalism, money and ego. Judging, as we will see in the next chapter, is a controversial area; it is very difficult to find five properly-qualified judges all of different nationalities.

Nationalism is a very human trait. Most judges will inwardly wish to give the riders representing their country a little extra boost. The few really qualified international judges control, to a great extent, the thinking of the less experienced judges who sometimes originate from countries where dressage is almost unknown.

A few years ago, I had the opportunity to ask one of the reigning foreign international judges how a certain newcomer to their ranks was faring as a judge. The answer I received was: 'Oh yes, that judge is faring well, but he is still having trouble placing the first five in the right order.' This brings me to the 'red line'; the demarcation that separates the first ten horses in the world from the rest of the field. In order to earn a spot among this elite company, you need a very good horse, and you have to plan to compete for long periods in the big international shows of Europe, and particularly those of Germany, the present mecca of dressage. You have to earn your reputation under fire before the judges will feel comfortable about rewarding you with high placings and wins. A relatively unknown horse − rider combination will take longer to achieve success than a well known rider with an unknown horse. Over the last twenty years of competition, there have always been one or two horse who have been outstanding and proven unbeatable in the eyes of the judges. Since this small field of horses reappears year after year in front of the same small group of judges, it is no wonder that competition at this high level is so very often prejudged.

Finances of Dressage: Maintaining the Art

When we have to travel with horses to distant locations, not only are there hardships involved, but a great amount of money is needed to make the whole project possible. Dressage is not a spectator sport that will ever attract big sponsorship, therefore, prize money will always be limited. I am sure that, in the future, clever promoters will devise new ideas and stage more inviting surroundings for dressage competitions. The electronic scoreboard, where the judges would have to punch in their marks, movement by movement, has been considered for years. Staging dressage competitions along with Grand Prix jumping; or dressage in association with other activities, in locations such as Disney World, or important performing art centres, might happen in the near future. Dressage will never become a spectator sport that will allow the competitor to make a very good living, and this limits the number of athletic talents who are willing to direct their physical and mental efforts to dressage when greater success and financial gain can be achieved in more popular sports.

Ego is the last detainment to the preservation of classical equitation and its integrity. This usually acts in two ways. You can arrange to purchase one of the top five horses in the world for an outrageous price payable in hard currency, or you can purchase ten outstanding five-year-olds each year and, through training schedules and methods that would be widely accepted in commando schools, come up with your own 'survival of the fittest' development programme. No doubt, a great horse will emerge from such training every now and then. I would venture to lay my money on the betting line at odds of twenty to one. I have discussed this philosophy with a few of the very best professional trainers in the world and their answers were un-animous; 'if horses cannot hold up to this approach, they will never make it to the highest levels under any circumstances anyway.' These professionals are business oriented and do not wish to waste time and money on horses who are not going to bring them the greatest rewards. I tend to agree with their business sense, but I do not agree with their lack of compassion for nature and youth, for I am sure that many nice horses are lost to this practice. If a person does not enjoy the daily discipline required to train horses, and the almost religious feeling with which a correctly trained horse will reward his rider day after day, then I say that person will never be a great rider, or trainer of horses. That person has missed the boat...

When a horse is classically developed and ready to be shown internationally, competition should be his verification. If the results of training are true art, he will win eventually under all judges. If his training is forced, and he is robotic and brainwashed, he may win some events but, not being artistic, will soon fade into oblivion.

CHAPTER 37

Judging

UNFORTUNATELY THIS SUBJECT CAN BE ONE OF the most frustrating aspects of our sport. Most judges are like eunuchs; they know how, but they can't. A good judge should be able to act not only as a critic, but also as an advisor and instructor, to help the competitor further the training and progress of his horse by offering knowledgeable comments and advice. To be effective in this process, a judge must have trained and competed successfully at the level he is judging. To quote Alois Podhajsky:

> As a judge I have on various occasions been confronted with the difficulties of this responsibility and I have come to the conclusion that not every rider is necessarily a good teacher, or a good judge. However, it is impossible for a man to be a good judge if he has not been a good rider in the category which he has to judge.

In my opinion, a first-rate judge must not only have competed successfully at the level he is judging, but he must also have a thorough theoretical knowledge, two good eyes and a very good memory. If these qualifications are not enough, let me add a few character testers such as; complete impartiality, honesty and compassion. Impartiality and honesty are self-explanatory. Compassion is an inner feeling that makes one hope the competitor will do well.

Another important attribute is positive judging; a willingness to award a good mark when it is deserved. There is nothing worse than negative judging when a judge looks only for faults, picks away at small errors, and never really sees or understands the overall performance. Such judges rarely have the courage to reward a good movement with a good mark. Their incompetence is almost always expressed in the collective marks and their comments, if any!

Perfection is often sought and rarely achieved in dressage, so it would be unreasonable to expect judges to be exceptions to the rule. There are a few excellent judges in America and Europe who I am sure do not come close to meeting the prerequisites mentioned. Through the education process of forums, years of experience judging, and no doubt an extra helping of grey matter, these judges have proven themselves to be very capable over a period of time, and can be compared favourably to their peers who, more often than not, have successful competitive careers in their backgrounds. Good riders know when they have ridden a good test and obtained the most out of their mounts; they also know when things do not go so well. They do not blame the judges for their lack of success on a bad day; or even for that matter, on a good day. No matter how good you are, there can always be someone better!

In 1974, at the World Championships in Copenhangen, I was having breakfast with Colonel Thackeray, who was one of the judges, when the President of the Jury, the late Gustav Neblaeus, came down from his room and sat at our table. After some chit-chat, Thack said: 'Gustav, this glass of orange juice is a wonderful eye opener.' Neblaeus replied: 'Thack, you had better have a second one, you are going to need both your eyes today.' This humour certainly broke the ice! Neblaeus went on to make another wise observation: 'You know, it is amazing – when I came down for breakfast, every rider greeted me with a smiling nod and a 'good morning' – but do you know, this evening at dinner there will only be one rider with a smiling face in this dining room!'

From that time on, I always made a point of seeking advice from the judges I respected after the competition and, without exception, I always found them friendly, willing and eager to oblige, and in most cases their off-the-record comments have been most helpful. In Europe the relationship between judges and riders is a good deal more relaxed. They can intermingle socially with greater ease and even have dinner together (providing the judge pays for his own dinner). On many occasions, I have spent late nights over a few beers with fellow competitors and judges. These occasions were not only great fun, but gave me a much clearer outlook on competitive riding and improved my performances in the arena.

Politics and nationalism in judging certainly do exist, as any seasoned competitor has found out; but this practice is largely limited to poor judges. Many riders express their disappointment at scores and placings they receive when they start competing in international shows. However, these marks, more often than not, reflect poor preparation, lack of experience, and perhaps a good dose of nerves! When I first started competing in international dressage classes, I was surprised to be awarded better marks by the international judges than I had received from judges at home. This same observation was made by my teammate, Elizabeth Lewis, back in 1974. Such judges are more willing to give a high mark when it is deserved, as well as a very low mark when it is called for. They see the overall picture – quality of horse, training of horse, rider's ability and preparation. In national competition, the arena is still a training ground for riders and horses, a place to assess one's work in public in front of judges. In international competition, when you canter down the centre line, you are representing your country. You and your mount are expected to have achieved the highest degree of perfection attainable and be ready to perform at the highest level of proficiency.

Years ago, I was practising at Cypress Point in Pebble Beach during the Bing Crosby National Pro-Am Golf Tournament. I must have hit 500 balls at my poor caddie, dutifully positioned at the bottom of the first fairway. I was trying to cure a bad fade that developed in my swing during first round play. The afternoon was getting shorter, the light was following a big red sun dipping into the Pacific Ocean. My hands were sore, my back ached, my swing was getting worse and my frustration was about to get the better of me when a little Scot walked over to where I was practising, looked me square in the eyes and said 'Laddie if ye did not bring it with ye, ye surely will not find it here.' He brought a smile to my face and we walked back to the club for a drink. How right he was! I should have been practising for the Crosby the month before, despite the cold weather in New York. I have never forgotten this advice and apply the philosophy to international dressage competition. Do not canter down the centre line until you are ready to meet the high standards required to win or place. To canter down the centre line only for experience will not enhance your reputation. Put your best foot forward only when you can win and meet the highest national standards at home.

The test of a good judge is not simply the ability to render marks on a score sheet, but to see the overall problems and strengths of a performance and give marks backed by knowledgeable comments which go to the core of the presentation.

Conclusion

THROUGH FATE AND CIRCUMSTANCE, I WAS REARED in France and, as a boy in his eighth year in 1936, I still remember the elegance and passion of the Cadre Noir performing in dressage exhibitions and jumping competitions in Paris at the Jardin D'Aglimatation. This encounter with equestrian sports left an indelible impression on my mind and soon led me to the Manège de Montevideo, where I was to spend most of my leisure time on and off over a period of nine years. My instructor was Mssr. Victor Laurent, a retired non-commissioned officer from Saumur and one of the finest trainers and instructors of his generation in France. The atmosphere of the school was typical of the 1930's; disciplined, formal, with great emphasis on dressage before all else. I was indoctrinated in the methods of Saumur, with strong emphasis on the teachings of François Baucher (1796–1873). Why Baucher, and not la Guérinière, the father of the French School?

During the years 1842–1843, General Nicolas Oudinot tried to introduce Baucher's methods to the French Army, but he was energetically opposed by Count D'Aure, then head of Saumur, who despised Baucher and considered him nothing more than a circus rider. François Baucher may never have entered the sacred walls of Saumur, but his methods did through his student General Alexis L'Hotte (1825–1904), who became commanding officer of the school in 1864 and established his own doctrine which combined the best of the exterior equitation principles of D'Aure, and the best of Haute Ecole by Baucher. Baucherism thus found its roots in the citadel of classical horsemanship. Why did Baucher have this influence on such a great artist as L'Hotte and others that followed him? I think that one may conclude that Baucher was alive and present, while la Guérinière was gone and somewhat forgotten in France. Baucher was no doubt a true artist; he was also a complete nonconformist, and his basic equestrian philosophy was very French. To Baucher, 'Equestrian science did not exist, it was to be created.' He advocated destroying all of the horse's resistances by direct and lateral flexions in place dismounted and ridden which, according to his method, brought about the contractibility of the horse between his hands and legs while creating an artificial balance which remained horizontal. He obtained complete lightness to his hands, or no contact at all. This method was logical, but above all easy to copy.

Please forgive me for this lapse into equestrian history, but it is an important observation as we will see later. After a few years at Montevideo, I turned my interest to showjumping and was instructed in the method of Colonel Danloux (1878–1945), who perfected the technical principles of the forward seat at Saumur, and strongly followed the natural method of Italy's Caprilli. This was my equestrian education – French to the core.

I later abandoned all serious riding and competition to pursue a career more suited to my family's wishes. I eventually returned to my first love of dressage in the late 1960's when living at home in Tuxedo, New York. France had by then dropped to a low ebb in world dressage, and Russia and West Germany were the two dominant countries. I decided to return to West Germany to learn as much about their methods and success as I could. Through the kind help and friendship of Ruth and Reiner Klimke, I purchased several good horses, and through them was introduced to the world of dressage and competition in Germany where I was given my second start.

At first I was amazed that the so-called German Method was completely based on the first French School of la Guérinière. Their horses, fitted with snaffle bridles, were ridden forward in one piece with impulsion. They were made very supple and strong throughout their bodies which resulted in a high degree of self-carriage and lightness. It became obvious to me that lightness was not the sole property of the Latin nations, but rather the domain of all riders, of any nationality, who possessed strong classic seats, the ability to coordinate their aids, and feel.

Trainers who persist in the constant use of the double bridle, and who place emphasis on achieving lightness by the collection of the horse's poll and the decontraction of his jaw, are lulled into a false sense of lightness which is short-lived because it does not originate from the horse's hindquarters, and, therefore, does not obtain the complete gymnastic development of the horse's body which alone results in true lightness and art.

So I can say, without hesitation, that I am the product of the second French School of Baucher and, thanks to my German friends, the first French School of la Guérinière. After years of experience in observing, training horses, competing and teaching, I can honestly say that the principles of la Guérinière have been more successful than those of Baucher; and for one simple reason – la Guérinière's approach to training was natural; Baucher's was not.

In essence most methods of training are sound if they follow the laws of nature. However, we must remember that the method can only be as good as the trainer. It is the trainer's character, temperament, intelligence, spirit and physical ability that, in final analysis, put the seal on the horse's development and performance.

National characteristics speak for themselves in international competition. A Latin will add flair, elegance and a sense of independence to a presentation, while his Tutonic brother will show discipline, correctness and a high degree of energy. These are simply inherited national traits. The best riders and and their mounts at this high level of competition will, without exception, show strength, suppleness and lightness.

If dressage is to grow as a spectator sport, it will have constantly to emit a beautiful picture of the horses and riders.

Knowledge of equestrian science is a necessity to train a horse. The execution of this knowledge can be taught. A good artisan will create a good product. Only an artist can create a masterpiece!

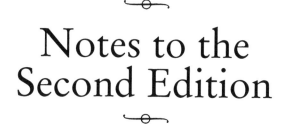

Notes to the Second Edition

CHAPTER 1 – THE RIDER'S SEAT AND POSTURE
Page 7.
All too often young children are taught to ride on ponies. As soon as they are old enough to be instructed, they should be taught on small horses. Ponies have choppy gaits and do not allow a young child to feel the correct gaits, rhythm, and cadence. Furthermore, the child will not develop the correct feel and balance as well as he would on a horse. First impressions are most important in this case; a child should learn the correct feel from the start and not have to graduate to it second-hand from the back of a pony.

CHAPTER 2 – CONFORMATION AND CHOICE OF A YOUNG
DRESSAGE PROSPECT
Page 13.
The European Warmblood breeders have made great progress in recent years. They have realized the need to breed a lighter type horse. As a result, an increased infusion of Thoroughbred blood has been used, whenever possible, to produce a more elegant and athletic horse.

Many breeders will only use mares sired by stallions whose offspring are successful in competition. They are also now more influenced by phenotype. *Webster's Collegiate Dictionary* defines phenotype as: "The visible properties of an organism that are produced by the interaction of genotype and the environment." Organisms with the same phenotype look alike but breed differently because of dominance.

It is therefore less important to think in terms of lines and more rewarding to analyze the entire pedigree to understand which ancestors have had the most influence on the final result. For instance, you may view a horse from the German "G" line and find few characteristics from that line but many of the characteristics from his dam's line.

Warmblood breeders today are, for the most part, broaderminded. They are willing to experiment and are not trapped in the singleness of mind the Trakehner breeders once were. The Trakehner breeders bred beautiful horses. Unfortunately, many of these horses had flat gaits, which at that time were considered the way a horse should move. Flat gaits, however, produce strong backs and a lack of elasticity. Athletic horses must move over at the knee. This movement, along with elasticity, is essential for jumpers and dressage horses to succeed at the highest levels of competition.

Some years ago, the Trakehner breeders recognized their mistake and are now trying to rectify the problem. It is not an easy task, for the Trakehner studbook is closed and the breeders are obliged to breed within their own bloodlines. When the Trakehner blood of the stallions Absatz and Abglanz appears in the Hanoverian lines back in the fifth and sixth generations of a pedigree, it has good influence, for it brings out the beautiful Trakehner type, without letting its genes overshadow the more athletic Hanoverian bloodlines within the pedigree.

CHAPTER 4 – BIOMECHANICAL ACTION OF THE VERTICAL COLUMN, THORAX, AND "POWER CURVE"

Page 30.

In recent years, the so-called "neo-classic" method of over-flexing the horse's neck and training very deep has had a direct relationship on the "power curve."

Excess in any form, as we know, is bad, and in most cases harmful. In the case of the so-called neo-classic method of hyper-flexion (extreme over-flexion of the horse's neck) made so popular lately by certain German riders, it would be wise to give this method of riding and training more thought.

Over-flexion was used by Plinzner at the Royal Stable in Berlin as early as 1874. His followers made excuses for his method, for he trained horses for Emperor William II of Germany, who had a severed arm and had to ride with one hand. This method allowed the Emperor to keep his horses on the bit. Baucher and Fillis also trained their horses by over-flexion of the neck. After World War II, this method of riding was used by show jumping riders from many nations. In recent years over-flexion has been made popular again by Dr. Uwe Schulten-Baumer Sr. and his riders. Their success in competition, no doubt, has influenced many trainers and riders to follow their lead.

Hyper-flexion is in complete opposition to the classic method of training a horse. Hyper-flexion when used by strong riders can be effective and a short cut to success in the show arena. Such riders are able to influence their mounts through from behind with strong driving aids, thus engaging the hindquarters and bringing up the horse's withers and back. Less talented riders who do not have as much influence on their mounts end up riding front to back, bringing up their horses' croups (not backs) and disengaging the hindquarters. Those in favor of hyper-flexion are quick to point out the success many recent riders have had using this method in the show arena, the most common example of which was Nicole Uphoff's Rembrandt, a difficult, spooky horse with a high head carriage. As Harry Boldt, her trainer, pointed out, "Whether one accepts a little mistake in the case of a very difficult horse in order to avoid a bigger on in the show ring does not mean that the entire way of riding has to change." This manner of training was successful and was done to benefit the rider's results in the show arena, not for the good of the horse.

The correct way to obtain a horse's back is the simple old classic way. Let the horse reach for the bit in a long frame. When he comes in contact and starts to chew the bit the rider may drive the horse forward and resist the forward motion momentarily with his hands until the horse releases the bit. Flexion is thus obtained of the poll with the horse's head slightly in front of the vertical. As I point out in my description of the power curve, normal flexion of the poll with tighten the nuchal and supraspinous ligaments sufficiently to lift the thoracic cage in the thoracic sling, allowing the muscles of the back, namely the latissimus dorsi, longissimus dorsi, and the gluteal group to oscillate, thus allowing the horse's top line to build muscle and suppleness, which, in turn, over a long period, will allow the horse to offer his back correctly to this rider when asked for collection.

Taking the short cut of hyper-flexion training has several ill effects on the horse. Ligaments have very little elasticity and over-extension can cause fiber rupture and pain. When the nuchal and supraspinous ligaments are over-stretched, too much pressure is placed on the bursas (small fluid-filled sacs) that help relieve and ease the movement of these ligaments across bony landmarks. Constant long-term over-flexion and pressure on these bursas will cause the horse to develop bursitis. Hyper-flexion also has ill effects on the horse's airways. Constant over-flexion and jamming of the throat-latch can cause respiratory problems and damage to the airways.

In training, false bends, over-flexion of the ligaments, and long compression of the horse's muscles are harmful and incorrect. These faults will result in the loss of true connection, impulsion, freedom of movement, and rhythm, not to mention the ill effects such actions have on the horse's mind.

In my opinion, whenever a horse is jammed together by a rider and the conversation becomes a one-way discussion, the rider can be considered no more than an artisan. When there is a two-way conversation and the horse has his say in the partnership, then and only then can the rider be considered an artist, for then an elegant and beautiful dance will be created, which when viewed, can be considered art.

CHAPTER 12 – THE CANTER
Page 52.
Transitions
The transitions walk-trot-walk will help the rider make sure that the horse is coming through properly from behind to the bit. The rider must feel the impulsion from the horse's hindquarters through his back and poll and onto his jaw. He must receive this transitional energy softly and through to the bit without any loss of impulsion or change of his head carriage.

These transitions, when asked for in dressage tests, call for three strides of walk. Almost every rider will execute the movement in three steps – not strides. One stride of walk has four steps, the rhythm of which is 1-2-3-4. Therefore, three strides must have twelve steps. This is hypothetical but it should be cleared up in the guidelines. I say this because the next most important thing to having the horse through in the downward transition is establishing the proper rhythm of the collected walk, and this cannot be accomplished in three steps.

Page 59.

The transitions canter-trot-canter ensures that the horse is coming through properly from behind. It also has a tendency to lower a horse's neck and is, therefore, a useful exercise for horses with high head carriages.

The transitions canter-walk-canter emphasize more collection and a greater degree of throughness. The proper rhythm of the collected walk must be established between the canter departs. For a discussion of the number of walk steps and their quality, see Chapter Twelve.

The transitions canter-halt-canter and canter-halt-rein back-canter will also ensure that the horse is supple, through, and in good self-carriage. These transitions, when repeated many times and intermingled (to prevent the horse from anticipating) help to improve the horse's canter stride.

CHAPTER 15 – LUNGING

Page 74

pany the horse up and down on a straight line parallel to the cavalletti, thus allowing the horse to turn on a wide semicircle. In the beginning I place three cavalletti at the lowest height, spaced at 1.40 metres (4.6 feet). This distance should be approximately right for the average horses' working trot stride, but as mentioned above, you must make sure that the horse's hind feet track in the middle of each cavalletto and make the necessary adjustments when needed. Here again, I make sure the horse looks for the ground, stretches his top line, and increases the flexion of his hindquarters. As the horse gains confidence on both reins, I gradually increase the number of cavalletti to six.

As the horse becomes more supple and stronger, I increase the height of the cavalletti to 30.5 centimetres (1 foot). At this new height you may have to readjust the width of the cavalletti to a shorter distance to accommodate a more collected trot stride. At this increased height I look for more cadence and greater flexion of the horse's hindquarters. I rarely use the highest setting of 40.5 centimetres (1 foot 4 inches) unless it becomes necessary to increase the flexion of the hindquarters.

This cavalletti work on the lunge brings about the utmost suppling and muscling of a young horse during his early training. I have found it to be better than ridden work over cavalletti at this stage, for the horse does not have to support the weight of the rider and can better use his back.

Later in training I have used cavalletti with success to improve a horse's lack of overstride in the extended walk, for a flat trot, and in developing the passage. The height and width of the cavalletti will very for this training. Each horse will require different adjustments. In dressage training this work over cavalletti must only be done at the walk and the trot. The canter cannot benefit from this form of training. It can only be beneficial when used for jumping exercises.

Chapter 29 – Pirouettes in the Canter
Page 140.
It is important in training pirouettes not to let the horse lose the engagement of his hindquarters and perform flat pirouettes in five strides or less.

When the horse is trained to perform pirouettes I continue refining the movement by asking for more engagement of the hindquarters and performing as many highly collected strides as possible in a working pirouette. To achieve this I increase my driving aids and restrain the side steps by lifting my inside hand. I usually can get between twelve to twenty strides, depending on the horse's physical ability.

By using this method of training, it is then easy to perform pirouettes in competition with very engaged hindquarters in eight well-balanced strides.

All too often we can observe in competition pirouettes ridden flat in five strides. In my opinion this is not artistic and does not bring out the ultimate beauty of the movement.

Chapter 30 – Developing the Piaffe In Hand and Ridden
Page 153.
The work in hand I had learned as a boy in France was based on the teachings of Baucher and Fillis. The horse was taught to come to the

whip. Side reins were not used. The trainer, dismounted, would hold the reins of the double bridle in one hand and with his other encourage the horse forward with whip aids administered to the horse's chest. When the trainer felt the horse responded well to this forward signal, he would start animating the horse's hindquarters by tapping his whip on the horse's croup and upper thighs. Making the horse come to the whip was very useful for teaching the movements of the Spanish walk and trot, canter and pirouettes on three legs, kneeling and bowing, but, as Fritz pointed out to me, this form of work in hand was circus training and had no place in classical dressage. The method I had learned as a boy simply made the horses piaffe with a high croup and a pronounced balance and loss of rhythm. I asked Fritz what a classic piaffer should look like. He smiled and told me the following story about Riding Master Polak at the Spanish Riding School.

One day a circus trainer visited the school and asked Head Rider Lindenbauer how they trained their horses in piaffer. Lindenbauer showed the trainer how work in hand was performed at the school. The circus rider was not impressed. "Anyone could work horses in hand," he said. Lindenbauer, being an industrious and very serious man, took affront to the visitor's comment. He called on Riding Master Polak to give this showman a mounted demonstration. Polak's mount, Favory Montenegra, had the best piaffer-passage at the school. Polak warmed up for a short time and then brought Favory Mantenegra to the center of the hall and performed a beautiful slow, elevated piaffer in perfect rhythm. The circus rider was still not impressed. He told Polak that any rider at the circus could do as well. Polak was a great talent who also enjoyed music and played the violin to perfection. He called on his groom to bring a metronome to the hall. "Now," said Polak to the circus rider, "set the instrument to any time you wish and my horse will piaffe to the exact rhythm. "Not bad," said the circus rider, "we will have to incorporate that act in our circus." Polak thought it time to teach this imposter a lesson. He asked his groom to fetch a glass of water and place it on Favory Montenegra's croup. "Now, young man, set the metronome," Polak said. "I will piaffe to its rhythm without spilling a drop of water." And so he did, demonstrating a classical piaffer, and adding, "try that at your circus if you can." Polak and Favory Montenegra then walked quietly out of the hall.

Fritz's point in telling me this story was to emphasize the great strength and suppleness a horse must attain to perform a correct piaffer. His strength and suppleness must be developed to the point at which the piaffer reaches such a degree of smoothness that it can barely be felt by the rider.

Only very talented and athletic horses can reach this high degree of training, but it should be every trainer's goal.

A Few Final Thoughts on the Piaffer

It is always very important to establish the comfort zone for each horse in the piaffer, both in hand and ridden. If the trainer asks for too much and leaves the horse's comfort zone, he will come into trouble and the horse's training will retrogress. On the other hand, if the trainer does not ask for enough, the horse will not progress. One must keep in mind that as training advances, the horse will be able to increase his tolerance for the number of piaffer steps he can perform.

The whip must always be used as an aid, not a punishment! The horse must respect the whip but must not be afraid of it. The less it is used, the better. The horse must always work in the utmost calmness and be returned to the stable in that state, so that when he returns to the site of piaffer training he will be relaxed and eager to perform again.

I cannot over-emphasize the importance of rewarding the horse with treats when he tries and performs satisfactorily, and of taking many rest periods during this work to keep him calm and attentive. Most all the horses I have trained in hand will piaffe in their stalls when I enter with carrots in my hand. Horses must be made to enjoy this taxing movement.

It is also very important for the trainer to remain calm and supple when walking or running backwards. His body must be upward and relaxed; any awkward movements on his part will distract the horse.

The trainer must also constantly observe the horse's back muscles to make sure they oscillate and do not become rigid. It is also important to keep an eye on the flexor and extensor muscles of the hind legs. If they tighten too much, the piaffer must be made more forward to relieve the pressure. The trainer must constantly make sure that the rhythm of the piaffer steps keeps the diagonal at all times. If the rhythm is lost the piaffer steps must be made more forward until the diagonal rhythm is reestablished.

Finally, when a horse is trained to piaffe properly under saddle, he should not be asked to piaffe more than twice a week. A little bit goes a long way. A horse can be soured out very quickly by over-training this highly collected movement and may eventually rebel against performing the piaffer altogether when asked to piaffe in the show arena.

CHAPTER 31 – PASSAGE
Page 155.
After World War II the Federation Equestre International (F.E.I.) revised its guidelines. During this time piaffer came under attack.

General Decarpentry of France wanted the piaffer to be considered passage on the spot, as did all the old masters. He reasoned that the piaffer must maintain the same diagonal rhythm, cadence, and elevation as the passage. He pointed out that if the exact rhythm was not maintained the executions of the transitions passage-piaffer-passage could not be performed correctly.

Dr. Gustave Rau of Germany wanted the piaffer to be considered a highly collected trot on the spot. He reasoned that horses could not lower their haunches sufficiently when brought back on the spot in the passage. Rau's interpretation of piaffer was adopted by the F.E.I. In my opinion this interpretation is misleading, for it opens the door for people to believe that here are two different rhythms and that the piaffer may be performed as a flat trot on the spot without the necessary rhythm, cadence and elevation that is required for a classic piaffer.

For the piaffer to be classical it must have the identical rhythm as the passage. This is one reason why it should be started in hand first, to slowly build sufficient muscles and suppleness, and to allow the horse to be able to flex the three joints of his hind legs and lower his croup when he is asked to piaffe on the spot.

CHAPTER 36 – COMPETITION
Page 177.
Some people erroneously believe that competition riding is different from classical equitation. It is not. Or, should I say, it should not be.

The F.E.I. guidelines were founded on classical principles that closely reflect Guérinière's thoughts. The old masters would have been in agreement with the F.E.I articles. Unfortunately, there are few horses today in competition that show the requirements of these articles. I refer primarily to the horse's frame, self-carriage, lightness, and acceptance of the bit. The current neo-fashion of hyper-flexion of the horse's neck does not encourage lightness and the relaxation of the horse's jaw. Placing the horse in an over-bent frame encourages a balance that favors too much weight on the horse's forehand and does not allow the complete flexion of his hindquarters and the lowering of his croup when asked for collection. These faults do not comply with the FEI's guidelines.

There were some disagreements when these F.E.I guidelines were revised after World War II, as I have pointed out in Chapter 31. Here again the format for competition came under fire.

General Decarpentry wanted to do away with the dressage letters and allow competitors to perform the required movements wherever they wished in the arena. He felt that this format would produce better artistic performances.

Dr. Gustave Rau, on the other hand, was in favor of keeping he letters emphasizing more demand on accuracy. The Germans won this point. This decision alone has had a vast influence on modern-day competition. Had France won out on that decision, competitive dressage may well have taken a more artistic venue.

Whether or not we like the F.E.I. guidelines or not is not the issue. We must live and die by rules, whether they be the Ten Commandments, the Constitution, or, indeed in this case, the rules and regulations of equestrian Federations. Perfection is rarely achieved, so it is only normal to find imperfections in all ruling bodies. The point is, we need a sound base to work from and the F.E.I. guidelines provide us with a platform.

The methods that do not follow the laws of nature are not classical. For instance, circus training cannot be considered classical, for it is artificial. The Spanish walk and trot, canter on three legs, pirouettes on three legs, canter and trot backwards, etc., are not natural movements for a horse and do not improve his gaits, suppleness, strength, or self-carriage.

Airs above the ground have been considered classical movements since the 16th century. In fact, Steinbrecht claimed they were the "peak of perfection of dressage." These classical movements do not improve a horse's gaits or suppleness, but they do increase his courage and strength.

It would be impossible to include airs above the ground in today's dressage tests, for very few horses have the conformation or physical ability to perform these exercises correctly. Perhaps some day the levade and pesade, which are the introductory exercises to the school jumps, will be introduced in the free style.

Competition riding can no longer be considered classical when short cuts are taken and force is used. When a horse is robotized through such training practices, his performances may be accurate, but the horse is robbed of his independence and true beauty. He will not show his true strength, lightness, and self-carriage.

Those who claim that there is a difference between classical equitation and competition are misled. In my opinion there is simply good training and riding, and bad.

Index

INDEX

INDEX

Pirouettes 105−6, 133−43
Podhajsky, Alois xvii, 181
Poles, Ground 73−4, 80
Posture 1−8, 69
'Power curve' 28−30
Preparation for competition 171−2
Psychology in training 16−23

Racing calendar 42
Reactions 18−19
Rearing 151
Rectitude 31−2, 56, 81
Rein-back 120−2
Renvers 33−5, 101−4, 139
Resistances 70−1
Retraining 75−7
Rewards 22, 146
Rhythm 46, 82, 98, 103−4, 109, 133−4
Rib cage 9
Ridden work 64−5, 150−3
Rubber snaffle 76

Saddle 79
Scapula 9−10
Seat 1−8
Seeger, Louis xvi
Self-carriage 4, 46
Semen, Frozen 14−15, 44
Senses 19−21
Sensitivity 22
Seunig, Waldemar xvii, 125
Shoulder 9−10, 105, 123
Shoulder-fore 91−2, 98, 108−9, 133, 140, 174
Shoulder-in 33−5, 89, 91−100, 102, 104, 108, 163, 167
Side reins 74−5, 146, 164
Sixth sense 16−17, 21
Smell 19−20
Snaffle bit 22, 78, 186
Spanish Riding School 102
Spirals 33
Steinbrecht, Gustav xvi, 90
Stensbeck, Oskar 161
Stiffness 80−1
    see also One-sidedness
Straightness see Rectitude
Strength 65
Stride, Lengthening 51
Stud book 42
Suppleness 37, 93, 135
    see also Flexibility

Surcingle 79
'Swing' 122

Temperament 146
Tempo 46, 48, 82, 98, 103−4, 109, 125, 133−4
Tesio, Federico 42−3
Thackeray, Col. 182
Thorax 27−8, 56−7, 89
Thorndike, Evie 175
Training, Psychology in 16−23
Training schedule 169−71
Traité d' equitation xvi
Transitions 80
Travel 171
Travers 33−5, 101−4, 167
Trot 12, 35−6, 50−4, 99, 166, 168, 173−4
    collected 50−1
    extended 52−4
    half-pass 107−9
    medium 52−4
    passage 154
    piaffe 147−9
    working 80
Turn on the forehand 95
Turn on the haunches 133

Vertebral column 25−7
Vision 20
Voice 70
Voltes 104

Walk 47−9, 147−9
    collected 47
    extended 47, 49
    half-pass 107−119
    medium 47, 49
    pirouette 133−4
Warming up 173−6
Webster's dictionary 44
Weight 8
Whip 145−6, 148−9
Withers 10

Xenophon xv

Young horses 9−15, 162, 173
    lungeing 73, 78−80
    riding 78−85

Zigzags 35−6, 109−111, 117−19, 167

∞ 202 ∞